Why is Julius Caesar a

Because he was one of history's great military commanders.

Because he freed Rome from a corrupt oligarchy.

Because he helped create the Roman Empire.

Because he gave his name to the world's most famous dynasty.

T.P. WISEMAN FBA was for many years Professor of Classics at the University of Exeter. He has written widely on Roman history and literature, including (with his wife Anne) a translation of Caesar's Gallic War commentaries.

525 194 24 0

JULIUS CAESAR

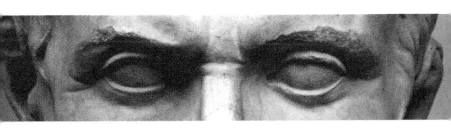

POCKET
GIANTS

T.P. WISEMAN

First published 2016

The History Press
The Mill, Brimscombe Port
Stroud, Gloucestershire, GL5 2QG
www.thehistorypress.co.uk

British Library Cataloguing in Publication Data.
A catalogue record for this book is available from the British Library.

ISBN 978 0 7509 6131 8

Typesetting and origination by The History Press
Printed and bound in the United Kingdom

Contents

1

The People's Thing

They are barbarians, but their system of government
is admirable.

Eratosthenes of Cyrene (c. 285–194 BC),
Greek philosopher and polymath[1]

Imagine a democratic state based on the rule of law. Citizens have equal rights, and contribute to the common wealth according to their means. Private extravagance is frowned upon, and legal safeguards protect the weak from the abuse of power. Now imagine a huge influx of wealth in the space of a single generation. Unprecedented economic inequalities follow. The rich get richer and come to believe that their interests and privileges are what the state exists to protect. Public assets are privatised, with legal safeguards and regulations ignored or evaded. Social tensions become acute. The old ideals of consensus and co-operation seem helpless against the greed and luxury of a powerful few.

That was the state of the Roman Republic when Gaius Julius Caesar was born in what we call 100 BC.

• • •

The Romans had been equals from the very beginning. They believed that Romulus, the founder of the city, had divided what little territory he then commanded into equal lots, and thus created 'maximum equality for all alike'.[2] Refugees came from elsewhere; no questions were asked, and to all who stayed he gave citizenship and an equal share in any new land won in war.[3] As the years went by there was no shortage of that.

Romulus did not found a dynasty. His successors, like him, were chosen by election and ruled by popular consent – until the seventh in the sequence, Tarquin 'the Arrogant', seized power by murdering his predecessor and dominated the Romans by armed force. This exception proved the rule: Tarquin and his clan were driven out of the city by a popular rising in 507 BC. The leader of the liberation movement was called Lucius Brutus.

Because of Tarquin, the Romans swore they would never have another king. What they put in place was defined as 'annual magistracies, and obedience not to men but to the laws'.[4] We call it the Roman Republic, borrowing the Latin phrase *res publica* (originally *res populica*), which meant 'the People's thing'. But no sooner had one form of corrupt rule ended than another began.

By 500 BC Rome had become a prosperous city state but her egalitarian ethos was under threat. Some families now defined themselves as 'patricians', meaning roughly 'those who know who their fathers were', and this self-appointed aristocracy of birth claimed a monopoly on public office. Patrician magistrates failed to protect plebeians (as the rest were now known) from exploitation and even enslavement by patrician landlords and creditors. The plebeians' response was to elect their own representatives, known as 'tribunes', who would protect individuals and veto any measure they considered abusive. The persons of the plebeian tribunes were declared 'sacrosanct': anyone offering violence to them would be regarded as an offender against the gods and therefore subject to summary execution.

A long stand-off followed, until in 367 BC the patricians' political monopoly was ended in a power-sharing agreement. Greek observers were enormously impressed by the fact that it had been achieved without bloodshed. As one of them put it much later:

> The People of Rome and the Senate were often in conflict with each other, both about legislation and about debt-cancellation, land-distribution or elections. But there was no civil violence, only lawful differences and arguments, and even those they settled honourably by making mutual concessions.[5]

What mattered was 'equal freedom for all',[6] and the achievement of it was what made the Roman Empire possible.

Within four generations of the power-sharing deal, the Romans controlled, by conquest or treaty, the whole of Italy south of the Apennines. Throughout the peninsula, good farming land was divided up into equal lots for Roman settlers. Seven *iugera* (about 1.7 hectares) was the standard size, and, as one commander put it, wanting more than everyone else got was the sign of a bad citizen.[7]

Three generations later, after two long and terrible wars with Carthage, the Romans controlled the whole western Mediterranean. In the second war they had been up against Hannibal, second only to Alexander the Great as a military genius. The two commanders who did most to defeat him (Fabius and Scipio) were both patricians; but the plebeian historian of those great events made a point of not naming the commanders.[8] It was the People's achievement – and when Scipio, as consul in 194 BC, instituted privileged seats for senators at the theatre games, it was regarded as an infringement of 'equal freedom':

> For 557 years [since the foundation of the city] the games have been watched by all together. What has suddenly happened to make senators not want to have plebeians among them in the auditorium? Why should a rich man object to a poor man sitting next to him? It's just a new and arrogant self-indulgence.[9]

The Romans still thought of themselves as a community of equals and now they were challenging kings. The great powers of the eastern Mediterranean were the dynastic monarchies that succeeded Alexander's short-lived empire: the Antigonids of Macedon, the Ptolemies of Egypt, the Seleucids of Syria, the Attalids of Pergamum. The first to fall was the oldest, Macedon.

The defeat and capture by the Romans of King Perseus, ninth in succession from Alexander himself, at the Battle of Pydna in 168 BC, was a truly epoch-making event. One indirect result of it was the presence in Rome of the Greek historian Polybius, who spent his years of exile writing a history to explain to his fellow countrymen:

> by what means, and under what system of govern-ment, the Romans succeeded in less than 53 years [220–167 BC] in bringing under their rule almost the

whole of the inhabited world, an achievement without parallel in human history.[10]

The 'system of government' was the key to understanding, and Polybius devoted a whole volume to describing the Roman republican constitution. Its excellence was demonstrated, he thought, by the citizens' moral behaviour: they acted in concord for the public good; they sacrificed their own interests to the welfare of the community; in office, they kept their oaths and were scrupulous with public funds.[11]

Confirmation of that judgement comes from another external source, the Jewish chronicler who narrated the revolt of Judas Maccabaeus against the Seleucid king Antiochus. In 160 BC, he reports that Judas had heard about the Romans: although their military power could make and unmake kings:

> not one of them made any personal claim to greatness by wearing the crown or donning the purple. They had established a senate where 320 senators met daily to deliberate, giving constant thought to the proper ordering of the affairs of the common people. They entrusted their government and the ruling of all their territories to one of their number every year, all obeying this one man without envy or jealousy among themselves.[12]

(In fact there were two consuls per year, but they held power in turn, alternating month by month.)

Together, Polybius and the author of *I Maccabees* provide an impressive testimonial to the virtues of 'the People's thing', the *res publica* of Rome's equal citizens, as late as the mid second century BC.

So what went wrong?

2

Greed and Arrogance

Greed destroyed honesty, integrity and all the other virtues, and taught instead arrogance, cruelty, neglect of the gods, and the belief that everything can be bought.

Gaius Sallustius Crispus (c. 86–35 BC),
Roman senator and historian[13]

Big money corrupts everything it touches, and it certainly touched the Roman Republic. Looking back a century later, in a time of civil war, Rome's historians identified a moral crisis: frugality and self-discipline had made Rome great; luxury and self-indulgence had brought her to disaster. And it happened because the huge influx of wealth from the wars of conquest did not benefit all Romans equally.

'To gain great wealth by honourable means' was always a legitimate ambition for Roman citizens.[14] Every five years they made a sworn declaration of the value of their property to the *censores*, senior magistrates whose duty it was to assess the financial, physical and moral health of the citizen body. That regular assessment was the basis of direct taxation: the richer you were, the more you contributed to the public treasury. But the appropriation of the King of Macedon's treasure changed all that. In 167 BC the direct taxation of Roman citizens was abolished, and the link was broken between private property and the common wealth.

What corrupted the Republic was not wealth in itself but the extent of it, and the arrogance of those who had it. Now that Rome had overseas territories to administer and exploit, a career in elected public office might mean not only the successive responsibilities of financial stewardship, judicial authority and military command, but also a year or more as a provincial governor, with unparalleled opportunities for self-enrichment, legal or otherwise, far away from the critical observation of honest citizens in Rome.

A new form of aristocracy now claimed special status – a 'nobility' defined as those who were 'well known' (*nobiles*) from forebears who had held high office. The most important magistracy, the consulship, came to be regarded by the *nobiles* as theirs by right:

> They passed it from hand to hand among themselves, and considered it a pollution if some 'unworthy' newcomer managed to get elected.[15]

It was the arrogance of the *nobilitas*, and popular resistance to it, that led directly to Rome's civil wars.[16]

Wealth had to be invested in land; consequently huge wealth meant huge properties. The Roman People owned extensive territory in Italy, much of it confiscated from allied communities who had backed Hannibal in the second Carthaginian war. Rents from these lands were an important public revenue. Since it was easy for the very rich to buy out their neighbours and acquire large holdings to be cultivated by slaves, an attempt was made to control the abuse by legislation. A law brought in by a plebeian tribune made it illegal for anyone to hold more than 500 *iugera* (about 125 hectares) of public land. That was more than seventy times the size of what had once been judged enough for any good citizen. Even so the law couldn't be enforced. The rich simply ignored it, and used their enormous holdings as if they were ancestral estates.

In 133 BC a more determined tribune, Tiberius Gracchus, proposed the confiscation of all public land held in excess of the legal limit, and its division into smallholdings for landless citizens. Public property, he said, should be for the benefit of all; it was not a good custom that anyone should possess more land than he could cultivate himself.[17] One of his colleagues tried to veto the proposal, but Gracchus got him deposed by popular vote, on the grounds that the People's tribunes should not go against the People's will.

The law passed, but the legislator did not survive. A group of hard-line *nobiles* – themselves, of course, great landholders – declared that the very existence of the Republic was under threat, and beat Gracchus to death. It was sacrilege as well as murder, unprecedented in Rome's history – a sacrosanct tribune openly killed in the lawful exercise of his office – and yet no one was held to account for it. On the contrary, when the Senate held an inquiry into the event, the outcome was the summary execution or banishment, without trial, of many of Gracchus' supporters. A dominant oligarchy evidently believed that the laws were for other people; *they* would decide what was in the interests of the Republic, and act as they saw fit.

After that, nothing could be the same again. Once murder had been used for political ends, and not punished, there was no going back.

The next victim was Gracchus' brother Gaius. In 123 BC, as tribune he organised the systematic taxation of Rome's new province of 'Asia' (western Turkey, in modern terms), once the Kingdom of Pergamum before King Attalus forestalled conquest by bequeathing it to Rome. This windfall was going to be for the Roman people as a whole, not just for a few profiteers. Another Gracchan law set up a publicly funded system of grain distribution at a guaranteed fixed price to protect ordinary citizens from hardship or debt exploitation in times of scarcity.

This time the oligarchs waited until Gaius was out of office, and obtained a senatorial resolution instructing the magistrates to 'protect the Republic', without reference to the laws.[18] The Senate's powers were never more than advisory, and the laws forbade the killing of Roman citizens without trial or appeal. It was an illusion of legal authority, but all they needed to justify armed force against Gaius Gracchus. He killed himself to avoid capture.

These events produced a sharp polarity in Roman politics, a new reality that two generations later was simply taken for granted:

In this state there have always been two sorts of people who have been ambitious to engage in politics and distinguish themselves there. They have chosen to be, respectively, by name and by nature either *populares* or *optimates*. Those who wanted their words and deeds to be welcome to the multitude were considered *populares*, and those who acted so as to justify their policies to all the best people were considered *optimates.*[19]

At the time this was written, Cicero was no friend of the popular cause. But he was honest enough to recognise, in a different work, that cliques of oligarchs called themselves *optimates.*[20]

From now on we can use this vocabulary to describe the two sides in an ideological struggle. The literal meaning of *optimates* is 'the best', like *aristoi* in Greek (whence 'aristocracy' as 'rule of the best'), but it is important to remember how tendentious the term was. Gaius Gracchus had it in mind when he pointedly called the men who killed his brother *pessimi* ('the worst').[21] *Populares* was a more transparent label, referring to people who believed in the old egalitarian *res publica*, 'the People's thing'.

We can hear the *populares'* indignation in a speech to the People by a plebeian tribune in 111 BC, attacking the corrupt oligarchs who had killed the Gracchus brothers and executed their supporters without trial:

Who are these people who have taken over the republic? Criminals with blood on their hands, insanely avaricious, utterly guilty but utterly arrogant, men who use honesty, reputation, loyalty – everything, good or bad – for profit. They've killed your tribunes, they've set up unjust tribunals, and they've strengthened their own position by slaughtering *you!*[22]

Soon the *optimates* were weakened by bribery scandals and military incompetence; so much so that in 108 BC a man of comparatively humble origin, Gaius Marius from Arpinum, was elected to the consulship to finish off a war in North Africa, previously botched by aristocratic commanders.

Marius was re-elected for an unprecedented run of five consecutive consulships (104–100 BC) because Italy itself was now threatened with invasion by two migrating Germanic peoples, the Cimbri and Teutones. By recruiting from a much wider social base than his predecessors, Marius evidently had a point to make: the legions *he* commanded would represent the whole range of the citizen body, including the poor and landless. If they were victorious, they would get the land they had fought for, just as in the old Republic.

But this enemy was something Rome had never faced before. Whole 'barbarian' peoples were on the move, tens of thousands of fighting men with their women and children in huge wagon trains, roaming Europe to find fertile land in which to settle. They had already seen off four Roman attempts to deter them; the last time, at Arausio (Orange) in 105 BC, had been the worst Roman defeat for over a century. The fertile land they wanted was the great plain between the Alps and the Apennines, 'Gaul this side the Alps' as the Romans called it.

In 102 BC they approached it separately, the Teutones from the west (modern Provence), the Cimbri from the north (modern Austria) over the Brenner Pass. Marius, consul for the fourth time, took on the Teutones and destroyed them at Aquae Sextiae (Aix-en-Provence), but his aristocratic colleague Quintus Catulus failed to stop the Cimbri as they came down the Val d'Adige. Soldiers and civilians alike fled in terror: 'The barbarians flooded into the empty land and plundered it.'[23]

The Cimbri now controlled all the rich territory from the Alps to the River Po. Only Marius could win it back. He did so in 101 BC, as consul for the fifth time, destroying the Cimbric horde at the Battle of the Raudian Fields (probably near Rovigo). Catulus was second-in-command, and with typical optimate arrogance claimed the credit for the victory himself. But the Roman People knew who had saved Italy from the barbarians: 'As they celebrated at home with their wives and children, they all made thank-offerings to Marius as well as to the gods.'[24] They then elected him to the consulship yet again.

Not all aristocrats were greedy oligarchs. Marius himself had married Julia, a lady from a very old patrician family, the Iulii Caesares, who claimed descent from the goddess Venus. Julia's brother served on the commission responsible for distributing land to needy citizens, including Marius' veterans. His own wife, Aurelia, gave birth to a boy during Marius' sixth consulship. The child was named after his father: Gaius Julius Caesar.

3

A Young Man to Watch

There are many Mariuses in that boy.

Lucius Cornelius Sulla (c. 138–79 BC),
Roman patrician and dictator[25]

We know nothing of Caesar's childhood, but his mother Aurelia was given the credit for his excellent education, and the conspicuous purity of his Latin was attributed to his home environment.[26] The Romans believed that speech mirrored character[27] and since Caesar grew up to be one of the finest orators of his time, the judgement of experts on his style of speaking – forceful, incisive, energetic, straightforward, noble – was equally a comment on his true nature.[28] He was tall, strong, well trained in the use of arms, and from first to last an old-fashioned *popularis*.

By the time Caesar came of age, the People's cause had suffered some serious setbacks. His uncle Marius may have saved Italy, but as soon as the crisis was over the optimate oligarchy struck back ruthlessly by murdering two elected tribunes. One was allegedly a son of Tiberius Gracchus; the other, a formidable politician called Lucius Saturninus, had pushed through a series of popular measures, including the one that distributed to poor citizens – and Marius' veterans – the broad lands captured back from the Cimbri in 'Gaul this side the Alps'. The Senate disputed the validity of Saturninus' laws, and hoped his fate would deter any future reformers. Once again, the rich and powerful protected their position with open violence.

Caesar was a babe in arms when that happened. He was 9 years old when the next tribune was murdered: Marcus Drusus in 91 BC. This time it was not done publicly (an unknown assassin, a knife in the ribs); but no one doubted the reason for it. In the hope of returning to Rome's traditional generosity with her citizenship, Drusus was proposing the enfranchisement of all the allied states in Italy. When he was killed, the resentful allies rose in arms against Rome.

It was a difficult and hard-fought war, with consuls killed in action in both 90 and 89 BC, and only the concession of the allies' demand brought it under control. The most effective of the Roman commanders was a patrician, Lucius Sulla. He was consul in 88 BC when the news came that Rome's province of 'Asia' had been invaded and the Romans resident there massacred. This was the one-time Kingdom of Pergamum, and the invader was another king, Mithridates of Pontus (north-east Turkey).

An army would have to be sent. Sulla naturally assumed he would command it, but the People decided otherwise. One of their tribunes that year was an eloquent young man called Publius Sulpicius, a *popularis* in the tradition of Saturninus and the Gracchi,[29] and on his proposal the People voted the command to their old hero Gaius Marius, now 70 years old but still fit and active.

What happened next took aristocratic violence to a whole new level. Sulla left the city and went to where his army of the previous year was still besieging a rebel stronghold in Campania. He resumed command of it, and marched on Rome with six legions. 'I shall free the city from tyranny,' he announced.[30]

The defence forces raised by Sulpicius and Marius did their best, but were overwhelmed in the streets of Rome. Early next morning, 12-year-old Gaius Caesar was no doubt with his father in the Forum to hear the consuls, with their military escort, explain to the Roman People how things were going to be. 'Equal liberty' was abolished: all voting henceforth would be in an assembly defined by property class, the richest voting first. No proposal would be put to the vote without previous approval by the Senate. The tribunes would have no legislative function and no right of veto. Armed soldiers patrolled the streets. Sulpicius was in hiding, but they found him and killed him. Old Marius managed to evade capture and fled abroad. For a young boy learning how politics worked, it was quite a lesson.

The *optimates'* military coup could not, however, be made permanent. Sulla was soon off to fight Mithridates, which would prove a long, hard job. There was another civil war in 87 BC, when a grim and embittered Marius returned to take vengeance on his enemies. Now *optimates* too were being murdered, victims of the cycle of violence they themselves had initiated. But Marius died in January 86 BC, thirteen days into his seventh consulship. Lucius Cinna, a *popularis,* was now consul, and would be re-elected twice more, presiding over a brief period of stability before Sulla returned.

During those three years of precarious peace, young Caesar legally became an adult (at 14), lost his father (at

15) and married (at 16). He was Marius' nephew; his bride Cornelia was Cinna's daughter. It was a match with a message, and not everybody liked it.

Sulla returned in 82 BC, again with a battle-hardened army, and again there was civil war. This time he was determined to stay in power and make his aristocratic agenda stick. He revived a constitutional expedient first devised by the patricians in the early years of the Republic to keep the plebeians under control: the emergency appointment of a *dictator* (Latin for 'he who gives orders'), against whose authority there was no appeal. The *dictator*'s unchecked power had previously been limited to six months' tenure, but that was a nicety Sulla could do without. He would be '*dictator* for the writing of laws and the regulation of the Republic', and he would hold office until he was satisfied with the result.[31]

Sulla posted in public a list of citizens he disapproved of. Anyone named on this 'proscription' could be killed with impunity; if you brought in the head, for identification and public display, you would get a reward. The resulting death toll was 4,700, including about forty senators. Their property was confiscated and sold at auction, and their children debarred from holding public office.

In this atmosphere of terror, the young couple were in serious danger. Cornelia's dowry was confiscated and Sulla told Caesar to divorce her. He refused, and made himself scarce while well-connected relatives talked the *dictator* out of having him killed. No doubt they promised that the headstrong boy would become a good optimate. Sulla told them they were wrong, but let him be. Caesar was out of range anyway, serving as a staff officer in the not yet fully reconquered province of 'Asia'. At 19, he was doing what a young Roman aristocrat was expected to do: looking for some military action to make a name for himself.

Sulla's rule was the victory of the *nobilitas*. 'It is obvious,' wrote a contemporary, 'that the power struggle is between the lower orders and their betters, and that now, thanks to Lucius Sulla, everyone has his proper rank and dignity restored.'[32] So much for equality. With the tribunes' veto and legislative powers abolished, the optimate oligarchy would be able to run the Republic as it saw fit, without any inconvenient interference from the Roman People. But there was resistance. No sooner had Sulla retired from public life (79 BC), and died soon after, than one of the consuls, an aristocrat called Marcus Lepidus, began urging that the legislation be rescinded.

Caesar was in Cilicia (southern Turkey), the most remote and lawless corner of the eastern Mediterranean. He was 22 and already a highly decorated officer: in 'Asia' he had won the oak leaf crown (*corona ciuica*), awarded for saving a fellow citizen's life by killing an enemy on the field of battle.[33] He came straight back to Rome at the news of Sulla's death. Lepidus hoped to use him as a *popularis* ally; but Lepidus had already put himself at the head of a rebel army, and the last thing Rome needed was more civil war. Caesar declined the offer. The Senate, led by 'all the nobility' and 'the leaders and standard-bearers of Sullan domination', gave its backing to whatever executive action was deemed necessary.[34] Lepidus' forces were routed just north of Rome, and his followers dealt with as brutally as those of the Gracchi and Saturninus had been.[35]

Untainted by association with armed rebellion, the eloquent young war hero set about defending 'the People's thing' the proper way, by prosecuting those who were corrupting it for their own profit.

There was not yet a 'Roman Empire' in the true sense, but there were already many extensive overseas territories 'in the power of the Roman People', won by force of arms or by diplomacy backed by the threat of arms. Kings who knew their kingdoms might be next had no illusions about how the Romans achieved their power and wealth.[36] The Roman People didn't worry about that (their founder Romulus was, after all, a son of Mars), but they did expect their overseas possessions to be a source of income to the public treasury, for the benefit of the citizen body as a whole, and not merely a source of private plunder for the senators sent out to govern them.

As far back as 149 BC one of the People's tribunes had set up a standing court for the prosecution of extortionate governors; Gaius Gracchus later prohibited senators from sitting as jurors, but Sulla reversed that, and now ex-governors facing prosecution could rely on a sympathetic hearing from men who had done the same themselves or were hoping for the chance of doing so soon. When Caesar prosecuted Gnaeus Dolabella before the court in 77 BC, he had plenty of evidence and gave a great speech, but he failed to secure a conviction. The following year he went for another notorious profiteer, this time in a civil court, but again he lost his case.

Big money corrupts everything. The corruption was open and blatant,[37] and until Sulla's 'regulation of the Republic' could be reversed and the powers of the tribunes restored, greed and arrogance could never be controlled. As the *populares* strove for the cause of public accountability, the young patrician was making his mark:

> Caesar won a brilliant reputation and great popularity by his eloquence in these trials. He had an ability to make himself liked which was remarkable in one of his age, and he was very much in the good graces of the ordinary citizen because of his easy manners and the friendly way in which he mixed with people. Then there were his dinner parties and entertainments, and a certain splendour about his whole way of life; all this made him gradually more and more important politically.[38]

But there were still some years to go before he could legally stand for public office. It was time to return to military action.

Late in 75 BC King Nicomedes of Bithynia (north-west Turkey) died, having willed his kingdom to the Roman People. His neighbour to the east, Rome's old enemy Mithridates, was not going to let the annexation take place without a fight. Caesar was already in the area – but not yet free to act. He had been kidnapped by pirates in the north-east Aegean and was waiting for the ransom to be delivered. As soon as it was, and he got back to the mainland, he manned some ships, captured the pirates and had them executed, all under his own responsibility. When the war broke out, he and his recruits were there to help defend the province from Mithridates' forces. That was what he was like at 25 years old.

4

The Ladder of Office

Will you follow the proposal of Gaius Caesar, who
has taken what is called the *popularis* line in public
life? If you do, I shall have less cause to fear popular
attacks, with him as the proposer and guarantor of
the motion. If you don't, I think I may have trouble
in store.

Marcus Tullius Cicero (106–43 BC),
addressing the Senate as consul in 63 BC[39]

Every year the Roman People elected twenty quaestors, most of whom served overseas as deputies to the provincial governors, looking after the finances. The quaestorship was 'the first step of honour' (election to it made you a senator),[40] and you had to be at least 30 years old to hold it. The second step might be the tribunate (there were ten plebeian tribunes a year), or the aedileship (four a year) that required you to organise the public festivals in Rome – chariot races, theatrical shows – and was therefore very expensive but excellent publicity. The third step was the praetorship, a magistracy in the modern sense with judicial duties, but also carrying with it what the Romans called *imperium*, the right of military command. Since there were eight praetors elected every year, each new senator had a 40 per cent chance of making it to the level that qualified him to command troops and govern a province. After that the odds lengthened, with only two ex-praetors statistically likely to make the fourth and final step to the top of the ladder, the consulship.

On the rare occasions when the Roman People had the chance to vote a *popularis* politician into office as consul, they liked to keep him there by re-election (like Marius from 104 to 100 BC, and Cinna from 87 to 84 BC). The *optimates* resisted that – they liked to pass the consulship round among themselves, and Sulla had duly obliged them by making it illegal to stand for a second consulship until ten years after the first. When Caesar took the first 'step of honour' by election as quaestor, much of the Sullan legislation had been reversed, but not that particular restriction. If he made it to the top, as a man of his ability and ambition might expect to do, he would have one year to do what needed doing, and then the oligarchs would have it their own way again for another ten.

As it happened, bereavement enabled Caesar to show the People where he stood. Early in 69 BC Cornelia died, still in her 20s (they had one child, a daughter); and Caesar's aunt Julia died around the same time. At each funeral he gave a powerful public speech reminding the citizens that this young woman was Cinna's daughter, and this patrician lady Marius' widow. No public memorial existed for either Cinna or Marius. Sulla had declared them both public enemies, and had Marius' ashes thrown into the river. But Caesar made sure that Marius' portrait mask was prominent in Julia's funeral procession:

> There were some who protested at this, but the People shouted them down and applauded Caesar in glad admiration, that after so many years he had brought Marius' honours back into the city as if from the underworld.[41]

The support was there – the question was how best to exploit it.

Caesar served his quaestorship in Spain, but left early. The tribunes' powers had been restored, and Sulla's corrupt oligarchy was, for the moment, on the defensive. It was time to be in Rome. But first he had a visit to make on the way back.

What is now the Lombard Plain in northern Italy was then still 'Gaul this side the Alps', a province ruled by a proconsul. Since the defeat of the Cimbri, the wide and fertile lands north of the River Padus (modern Po) had been occupied by smallholders, largely Marian veterans and their descendants, who called themselves 'Transpadanes'. At first the legality of their holdings, which had been granted by Saturninus, was disputed; but in 89 BC they were officially recognised as 'Latin colonists', a status halfway to citizenship (only if elected to a local magistracy would you be enfranchised as a full citizen). Now that all Italy south of the Apennines enjoyed Roman citizenship (since the War of the Allies in 90–89 BC), the Transpadanes, proudly adhering to the old-fashioned values of the Roman Republic,[42] naturally resented their unprivileged position. Promising he would right the wrong when he got the chance, Caesar hurried on to Rome.

He couldn't be a tribune himself (as a patrician, he was ineligible), but he gave what help he could to the tribunes' reform programme. In particular, he was the only senator to support an ad hoc emergency command against piracy, with unprecedented authority over the whole Mediterranean. The People voted it into law against furious optimate opposition, and were immediately justified by the swift and brilliant success of their chosen commander, Gnaeus Pompeius ('Pompey the Great').

Pompey was only six years older than Caesar, but at 40 already the most experienced and successful military commander of his time. He had fought for Sulla in the civil wars, and for Sulla's oligarchy afterwards, but then lent his prestige and charisma to the restoration of the tribunes' powers in 70 BC. He wasn't interested in political ideology; what he wanted – and got in plenty – was applause and admiration.

Having destroyed the pirates' fleets and bases in a masterly campaign in 67 BC, the following year Pompey was given command of all the armies in the eastern provinces (three aristocratic commanders were recalled) in order to finish off, at last, Rome's tenacious enemy, Mithridates of Pontus. That too was a popular vote sponsored by a tribune in the teeth of senatorial opposition; and again Caesar spoke in favour.

Caesar's own bid for the People's favour came with his aedileship in 65 BC. Spending huge amounts of borrowed money, he put on a series of spectacularly lavish games in a purpose-built setting of temporary porticos in the Forum and on the Capitol. For the climax, he staged a special demonstration:

> He had portraits of Marius made in secret, along with statues of Victory carrying trophies. He took them to the Capitol by night and set them up. At dawn they could be seen glittering with gold and beautifully crafted, with inscriptions recording the

Cimbrian successes, and bystanders were amazed
at the audacity of the man who had set them up ...
The Senate gathered to discuss it. Lutatius Catulus,
the most respected Roman of the day, stood up and
denounced Caesar ... but Caesar spoke in his own
defence, and it was he who carried the Senate. That
encouraged his admirers even more, and they urged
him not to bow to anybody. He had the People's
support; with it, he would conquer everyone, and
win the highest place of all.[43]

Catulus was one of those 'leaders and standard-bearers
of Sullan domination' who had defeated Lepidus twelve
years earlier, son of the Catulus who had failed to stop the
Cimbri and then claimed the credit for destroying them.
He and Caesar respectively epitomised the optimate and
popularis views of what the Republic should be.

Two years later, in 63 BC, Caesar won two elections in
quick succession. One was predictable, for the praetorship,
the third rung on the ladder. The other was something
extraordinary.

Roman religious practice was looked after not by
a professional clergy, but by various priestly colleges
composed of senators. One of them, the college of
pontifices, was responsible for keeping the Roman People
informed about their duties towards the gods, and in
63 BC, on the proposal of a tribune, the People passed a
law that appointment to the pontifical college should be
not by co-optation, as Sulla had made it, but by popular
election. Caesar had been a member for about ten years,

and at just this moment the head of the college (*pontifex maximus*) died, meaning there would be an election for his successor. Two senior aristocrats, one of them Catulus, were assumed to be the only realistic candidates. The People elected Caesar.

It was a characteristic throw of the dice – all or nothing. After borrowing so hugely for the games, he had to prove to his creditors that he was something special. Fail, and they would bankrupt him. Caesar is said to have told his mother, as he left for the election, 'I shall return as *pontifex maximus*, or not at all.'

There was plenty of work for *populares* that year: tribunes' proposals for debt relief and land distribution (both defeated by the *optimates*) and, late in the year, just as in Lepidus' time, an armed uprising of impoverished and desperate smallholders. Again, the Senate passed a resolution encouraging executive action without reference to the laws, and in December the presiding consul, Marcus Cicero, asked what he should do with five men who had evidently been plotting a murderous *coup d'état* in the city. The vote went in favour of summary execution, as if the Senate had the powers of a court of law. Caesar spoke against this, and as he came out of the building the consul's bodyguard surrounded him with drawn swords. Cicero told them to let him pass but, according to the optimate view of things, he would have been entitled to give a different order.

A month later Caesar was making the most of his praetorship, co-operating with one of the tribunes in complaints against Cicero for allowing the killing of

Roman citizens without trial and against Catulus for embezzlement of public money in the rebuilding contract for the temple of Jupiter on the Capitol. As always, greed and arrogance were the targets.

The Senate reacted by suspending Caesar from his public duties. At first he took no notice, since the Senate had no constitutional right to impose such a restriction, but when threatened with violence he retired to his house:

Next day, the People flocked to his house of their own accord and enthusiastically offered their help to reinstate him, but he restrained them. The Senate, which had hurriedly met to deal with this disturbance, sent a delegation of senior members to thank him, and then summoned him to the Senate-house, expressed their appreciation in formal terms, and restored him to office by rescinding their earlier action.[44]

He had made his point. The People's view could not be ignored.

What mattered that year (62 BC) was the news from the East. Mithridates was dead, and victorious Pompey had gone on to organise the entire region as far south as Judaea, annexing in the process what was left of the Seleucid Kingdom of Syria. As he himself put it, he had brought into submission all the lands from the Crimean peninsula to the Red Sea, and increased the revenues of the Roman public treasury from 50 million to 135 million *denarii* per annum.[45] Pompey returned to Italy late in the year, confident that his arrangements would be ratified and his deserving veterans rewarded with land settlements. That did not happen. The *optimates* did not share the People's enthusiasm for Pompey, and for the next two years (61–60 BC) did everything they could to make life difficult for him.

Caesar, meanwhile, was in his praetorian province of 'further Spain', employing against the native peoples of Lusitania the traditional Roman imperialist tactic: provoke resistance and then conquer those who resist. With his usual energy and decisiveness he followed up by immediately raising a fleet from Gades (Cádiz) and sailing up the Atlantic coast beyond Finisterre, to receive the submission of the Callaeci in what is now Galicia. So he too had a fine report to send back: just as Pompey had conquered to the Red Sea, so Caesar had displayed Rome's power on the outer Ocean itself. That was what the Roman People wanted to hear – much better than the usual story of optimate proconsuls feathering their own nests. Caesar's booty (and there was plenty of it) went to pay off his creditors.

His year over, he left for Rome without even waiting for his successor to arrive. There was work to do: an election campaign to fight, a consulship to win and a *popularis* programme to put into action. To overcome the tenacious hostility of the optimate oligarchs, he would need all the help he could get, and there were three men in particular whose support he wanted.

One was Pompey, still unable to get the land bill for his veterans passed and his eastern settlement formally ratified. He needed a dynamic consul tough enough to beat down the opposition. Another target was Marcus Crassus, the richest man in Rome and, like Pompey, an ex-Sullan who had edged away from the *optimates*. He needed legislation to give his friends in the tax-farming business a more favourable contract. The trouble was, he and Pompey detested each other. The third man was Cicero, whose wonderfully persuasive oratory might be diverted away from the optimate cause. Changing sides would get him off the hook for putting Roman citizens to death without trial three years before.

Caesar won his election, with an optimate, Marcus Bibulus, as his unwelcome colleague. Cicero, thinking hard about what to do when they entered office, wrote to his friend Atticus in December 60 BC:

> Either (*a*) I must resist the Land Bill strongly, which would involve a certain amount of fighting but much increase my prestige, or (*b*) I must keep quiet, which means retiring to Solonium or Antium [two of his country houses], or (*c*) I must support it, which they say Caesar is quite convinced I shall do; for Cornelius came to see me – I mean Cornelius Balbus, Caesar's friend – and assured me that Caesar would consult Pompey and me about everything, and would make an effort to reconcile Pompey and Crassus. In favour of (*c*) are the following advantages: intimate connections with Pompey, and with Caesar too, if I like; reconciliation with my enemies; peace with the masses; and a quiet old age.[46]

He chose (*a*) and didn't get his quiet old age. Caesar was disappointed, but his diplomacy did succeed with the reconciliation of Pompey and Crassus. The three men agreed a formal alliance, pooled their resources and made their plans.

5

The Body Politic

What if I can make a better citizen also of Caesar, who has the wind in his sails just now? ... A cure which healed the diseased portions of the state would be preferable to one which amputated them.

Marcus Tullius Cicero, writing
to his friend Atticus in 60 BC[47]

Thanks to the extraordinary survival of large parts of Cicero's correspondence, the years from 61 to 43 BC are the best attested in the whole of Roman history. The letters are important for our story because they give us an insight into the assumptions of an optimate politician who was also supremely intelligent, cultured and articulate. One idea in particular is worth focusing on: the health of the body politic.

The metaphor of the state as a human body was traditional in Roman thought;[48] harmonious co-operation between the different body parts represented the give and take of non-violent debate and compromise that had so impressed Polybius and the author of *I Maccabees* a century before Cicero's time. But things had changed since their day.

Strictly speaking, the Senate was the *senatus populi Romani*, serving the Roman People and responsible to it.[49] The *optimates* thought that a feeble idea. They preferred to believe that the People had handed over the control and guidance of the Republic to the Senate.[50] Their view of the body politic was that only *they* could assess its state of health and decide whether the appropriate treatment was medicine or surgery. If the latter, then lethal violence could be used.[51]

What political disease could justify that sort of intervention? Two other frequently used metaphors provide the answer. Since the Republic consisted of free citizens, subject to no king or master, any power that could be described as *dominatio* (the authority of a master over slaves) or as *regnum* (the authority of a king over subjects) was necessarily intolerable. Besides, many wealthy Romans were educated well enough in Greek philosophy to know the classic analyses of tyranny in Plato's *Republic* and Aristotle's *Politics*, which seemed to justify the idea that to kill such a ruler was not only permissible but a moral duty. Even Cicero, humane and civilised as he was, could take it as self-evident that a 'tyrant' had forfeited the right to be treated as a human being: he must be 'removed from the common body of humanity' as a diseased limb is amputated.[52] So who would decide who qualified? That wasn't a problem for the *optimates*. They would.

It is only by bearing this context in mind that we can begin to understand the reaction to Caesar's programme as consul in 59 BC.

The first thing he did was set up a system for the recording and publication of the Senate's proceedings. The People should know what the People's senators said and did. Then he introduced a debate on the land bill, insisting that he would only bring in legislation that was in everyone's interests:

The swollen population of the city, which was chiefly responsible for the frequent rioting, would be turned towards labour and agriculture; and the greater part of Italy, now desolate [after the destructive slave revolt of Spartacus, 73–70 BC], would be colonised afresh, so that not only those who had toiled in the campaigns, but all the rest as well, would have ample subsistence.[53]

No one's estates would be confiscated or compulsorily purchased; with the profits of Pompey's great conquests, the public treasury would be well able to buy from the willing at the declared census valuation. This would be organised by a land commission of twenty senators, *not* including Caesar, and the Campanian land, closest to the wealthy senators' country seats, was specifically exempted.

The Senate could find no grounds for objection, but refused to back the bill. Their main spokesman was a personal enemy of Caesar, Marcus Cato, great-grandson of the historian who didn't name commanders (chapter 1). The elder Cato had been an outspoken traditionalist, championing the old republican virtues against luxury and extravagance, a consistent opponent of the wealthy aristocracy.[54] His descendant was equally austere in his morality, and equally hostile to innovation; but the effect of *his* intransigence was to protect the dominance of the luxury-loving aristocrats themselves: 'He had no fault to find with the measure, but nevertheless urged them on general principles to abide by the existing system and to take no steps beyond it.'[55]

Marcus Bibulus, the other consul of the year, was Cato's son-in-law. At a public meeting, Caesar asked him if there was anything about the bill he disapproved of. Bibulus wouldn't answer, except to say that he would allow no innovations in his year of office. Caesar turned to the People: 'You'll have the law, if only he agrees.' 'You won't have it this year,' Bibulus told them. 'Not even if all of you want it.' And with that he walked off.[56]

Having demonstrated the *optimates*' refusal to respect the People's will, Caesar went ahead anyway. Petty obstruction was swept aside, and the land bill passed without the benefit of senatorial approval. A few months later, a second bill was passed distributing the hitherto excluded Campanian land as well. Pompey's eastern settlement was ratified, Crassus' tax farmer friends got their contract revised, and now the revenues could start rolling in.

Cicero's letters complained of tyranny and enslavement. What he meant was that the wealthy landowners – whose spokesman he was – no longer had everything their own way.[57] Naturally, the body politic came into his mind: 'The state is dying from a new sort of disease. Although everyone disapproves and complains … no treatment is being offered.'[58]

The sort of treatment that might be applied became clear in August when an informer revealed a plot by a group of young aristocrats to kill Pompey. The *optimates* called it a false accusation, but, considering what their fathers and grandfathers had done to Tiberius Gracchus and Lucius Saturninus, it was perfectly credible.

At the heart of the crisis of the Republic lay a simple question: who was the Roman Empire *for*? More than a century had passed since the abolition of direct taxation, and it was now taken for granted by the Roman People that their treasury's main source of income should be the profits of empire. It is easy to see why Mithridates of Pontus, who resisted them for thirty years, described the Romans as 'the world's robbers' (*latrones gentium*).[59] Not many Romans cared about that, but they did care about who should benefit. Should it be the already rich, investing in great estates and the slaves to run them, or the common people, who fought the wars that brought in the revenue?

Extortion and abuse of power by senior senators governing provinces was a problem that had long been recognised but never adequately addressed. Now Caesar brought forward a comprehensive statute to regulate governors' behaviour. Though the Senate refused to discuss it, this was a truly foundational enactment, establishing the norms of Roman provincial administration for centuries to come.[60] The empire should be exploited rationally and for the (Roman) public good, with provincial taxes collected for the public treasury under contract for a fixed sum; it should not be an opportunity for office holders simply to amass private fortunes.

The optimate clique didn't like regulation, just as it didn't like land distribution. It expected to be able to prevent such legislation happening, and regarded as tyranny any limitation of its freedom to do so. Anger focused on Pompey as the most prominent of the three allies. In April of 59 BC Pompey had married Caesar's daughter Julia. Despite the thirty-year age gap it was a very successful marriage; but all the *optimates* could see was cynical opportunism. 'It is intolerable,' thundered

Cato, 'that political power should be prostituted by marriage alliances, and that men should help each other to magistracies, armies and commands by means of women.'[61] He was referring also to Caesar's own marriage to Calpurnia, whose father, Lucius Piso, was one of the consuls elected for the following year. Caesar would need a friendly consul while he was away fighting the People's war of conquest.

The Senate had hoped to neutralise the effect of Caesar's consulship by announcing that the consular provinces of that year would be the forests and drove roads of Italy – in effect, a police job putting down rural banditry. But once again the People defied the Senate and imposed its will. On the proposal of one of the tribunes, Caesar was granted a special command, for five years, over 'Gaul this side the Alps' (welcome news to the Transpadane settlers, still eager for full citizenship) and Illyricum along the north-east Adriatic coast (modern Slovenia and Croatia).

The plan was evidently to conquer the lands of the Danube, where a charismatic leader called Burebistas had built up a powerful coalition of peoples,[62] but there was another option too. The conquest of 'Gaul beyond the Alps' (modern France and Belgium) would save Italy from the kind of terror the Cimbri and Teutones had caused in the past. So Pompey proposed in the Senate that Transalpine Gaul be added to Caesar's command.

The Senate agreed. Had they given up the struggle or were they playing a more devious game? If Caesar were to campaign in Gaul, he would soon come into conflict with a German warlord called Ariovistus who was expanding his territory across the Rhine into southern Alsace. Some very distinguished Romans were in touch with Ariovistus. They would be grateful, their emissaries told him, if Caesar could be killed.[63]

6

To the Ocean and Beyond

How pleased I was to get your letter from Britain!
I dreaded the Ocean and the island coast ... You
evidently have some splendid literary material –
the places, the natural phenomena and scenes, the
customs, the peoples you fight, and, last but not
least, the Commander-in-Chief!

Marcus Tullius Cicero, writing
to his brother Quintus in 54 BC[64]

What was so special about Caesar? Other men were clever, able, ambitious, charming and ruthless – but Caesar was all that and more. What made him different was his extraordinary vigour, decisiveness and power of concentration.

Whatever he needed to master, he mastered thoroughly. We happen to know, for instance, that his letter of instruction to the commissioners administering the land law began by explaining the origins of the science of land surveying.[65] His mental energy was astonishingly focused. He would go on reading and writing while dictating letters or listening to reports being read to him, and when necessary he would dictate four items of correspondence simultaneously, to four different secretaries.[66] Whatever the situation he was faced with, Caesar had in his head the information he needed and was ready to act on it without a moment's hesitation.

He needed all that multitasking power in the winter and spring of 59–58 BC. He had to appoint his senior officers (the People had given him the right to hand-pick them), arrange for recruitment in his province (he knew he would need more than the four legions officially approved), and receive and act on information brought from far beyond the territories of Rome. Was the danger from Burebistas'

Danubian league urgent or not? The Helvetii were going to abandon their territory in Switzerland and migrate to the Atlantic coast; could they be trusted not to turn south as the Cimbri had done? And all the while Caesar needed to keep his attention on a very tricky political situation.

One of the tribunes elected for 58 BC was a high-profile young aristocrat with a radical *popularis* agenda. He was Publius Clodius, a patrician Claudius who spelt his name differently for the sake of street-credibility. Patricians were disqualified from election to the tribunate, so Clodius had had himself adopted by a plebeian. Since that required a religious sanction, the *pontifex maximus* had to approve it. Caesar had done so, no doubt calculating that the value of Clodius' political projects would outweigh the dangers of his maverick style.

What made it complicated was that Clodius was a deadly enemy of Cicero, who had destroyed his alibi in a notorious court case not long before, whereas Caesar still hoped to get the golden-tongued orator on his side. Clodius now brought in a law pointedly restating the traditional principle that no Roman citizen could be put to death without trial, as Cicero, on the Senate's authority alone, had done in 63 BC. Evidently the Roman People could expect his immediate impeachment and condemnation. Caesar did his best for Cicero. He had already offered the protection of a place on his staff, and now he publicly deplored Clodius' retrospective legislation; but it was too late. Cicero decided to jump before he was pushed and in mid March left Rome to go into exile. At last Caesar could move, and he had to move fast.

Three of his four legions were at Aquileia, on the north coast of the Adriatic, ready to march east and south into Illyricum. But the immediate danger was 400 miles away across the Alps, where the Helvetii were preparing their wagon trains for the great trek west. There was just one legion in that part of 'Gaul beyond the Alps' that Rome already controlled (Provence, so called from the Roman 'province'). Lake Geneva and the Upper Rhône formed the northern boundary; but now the Helvetii wanted safe passage through Roman territory on their way to their new home.

Within eight days of leaving Rome Caesar was at Geneva, his legionaries were dismantling the bridge and a 19-mile fortified barrier was being constructed from the lake to the Jura Mountains. Having bought time by pretending to consider the Helvetic leaders' request, Caesar hurried directly back across the Alps to take command of the three Aquileia legions, already on their way west, and two more that had been raised on his own initiative – and at his own expense – from the Transpadane settlers, descendants of Marius' veterans called up to do what their fathers and grandfathers had done in 101 BC.

Now with a substantial army, Caesar returned to the Transalpine province via Mont Genèvre, and marched quickly north in pursuit of the Helvetii. They had crossed the Jura Mountains north of the Roman fortification and were already west of the Saône. Caesar bridged the river and followed with all six legions. The decisive battle took place near the Aeduan tribal capital of Bibracte (not far from Autun in Burgundy), far beyond the boundary of the Roman province. Defeated, the surviving Helvetii were sent back to their abandoned homeland, while Caesar, acting on information from the Aedui and other Gallic peoples, planned his campaign against the German chieftain Ariovistus.

That took his army even further afield, first to Vesontio (Besançon), tribal capital of Ariovistus' vassals, the Sequani, and from there to the Vosges Mountains and the Upper Rhine. It was probably somewhere south of Strasbourg that Caesar forced the Germans to fight, defeated their entire forces and pursued the survivors into the river.

In just six months since his hurried departure from Rome, Caesar had carried out two spectacularly successful campaigns. But that was just the start. He pointedly did not bring the legions back to the Roman province, but established them in winter quarters at Vesontio. The People had given him a five-year command, and he would soon be back to continue it.

Meanwhile he had other work to do, as magistrate in the assize towns of 'Gaul this side the Alps'. He probably went first to Lucca, the southernmost urban centre in his province, from where communication with Rome was relatively swift and easy. He needed to get the latest news from his ally and son-in-law Pompey, who was furious with Clodius. The tribune had gone out of his way to humiliate him, even posting armed guards outside his house to prevent him appearing in public; as such Pompey now wanted to get Cicero recalled.[67]

Constantly active, Caesar was recruiting again. Two more legions raised from the faithful Transpadanes would pay for themselves in the next stage of conquest. Even while he presided in court at each of their colonial centres (the future cities of Milan, Brescia, Verona, Vicenza, Padua), he was composing the first of his reports to the Roman People. A later biographer described him in action:

> As he drove to each of the fortresses, towns and camps, he had sitting next to him just one servant, trained to take dictation while on the move, and standing behind him just one soldier with a sword.[68]

Not for Caesar the grand entourage of a typical proconsul. He needed to get things done, and we can be sure the long, detailed and brilliant narrative known to us as 'Book One of Caesar's *Gallic War*' was finished, copied and distributed in good time for the first of the Roman 'theatre games' on 4 April.

Ordinary Romans were very keen on history.[69] Not from books, of course, which were far beyond their means (papyrus was expensive to import, copyists expensive to employ), but from occasions when they had the chance to hear it being read to them. So Caesar's distribution of copies for public recitation was just another aspect of his famous generosity.[70] In Rome the theatre games were where the whole populace came together,[71] and equivalent festivals must have provided enthusiastic audiences in the other towns of Italy as well. Caesar held his command by authority of the Roman People alone, and it was to them, directly, that he would report what he was doing with it.

His second year of campaigning saw the conquest of the Belgic peoples north-east of the Seine and the Marne. Caesar needed all eight of his legions in action to survive their combined onslaught at the River Sambre, a desperate affair that could easily have brought his whole adventure to an end. But at the start of the following campaigning season (April 56 BC), when audiences in Rome were already enjoying his thrilling story of that battle, Caesar was still in Italy, holding serious political discussions with Crassus at Ravenna and with Pompey at Lucca.

Cicero had been recalled and was back in action in the optimate cause; Clodius was using street violence to stir up trouble for Pompey, apparently with Crassus' connivance. The *popularis* coalition was breaking apart and it was time for a call to order. Caesar got his allies to agree a new political strategy: Pompey and Crassus would get themselves elected consuls for 55 BC and then arrange for the People to vote on three more five-year special commands.

Pompey would get Spain, with permission to command by proxy and remain in the vicinity of Rome. Crassus would get Syria, from where he could launch the great campaign of conquest he had always hankered after, over the Euphrates against the Kingdom of Parthia (modern Iraq and Iran). Caesar would get a further five years added to his existing command, giving him time to take on the Danubian project too. After that, the legally required ten-year interval having elapsed, he would hope to be consul again and once more protect the People's interests in person.

So it was agreed. Cicero was told firmly that, since Pompey had got him recalled from exile, he had better show his gratitude by co-operating. Caesar went back north to subdue the peoples of Normandy, Brittany and Aquitaine. After a long struggle against furious optimate opposition, Pompey and Crassus were eventually elected as consuls, and one of the People's tribunes duly delivered the necessary legislation.

In the fourth season of what would be a ten-year command, Caesar sought new horizons. He had extended Rome's dominions as far as the great Ocean, from the Pyrenees to the Rhine delta. Now it was time to go beyond.

First, to Germany. Having attacked and expelled two German tribes who had crossed over into Belgium, Caesar decided to take his own army across the Rhine, and to do it in the most impressive way possible, by building a bridge. The reason was simple:

> I could see the Germans were all too ready to cross into Gaul, and I wanted them to have reasons of their own for anxiety when they realised that an army of the Roman People could and would cross the Rhine.[72]

He made his point by burning buildings and destroying crops at will, and after eighteen days led his forces back across the bridge and destroyed it behind them.

Next, to Britain. It was late summer, but there was still time for an even more spectacular demonstration of Roman power – by crossing the Ocean to reconnoitre an unknown land:

In the ordinary way no one goes to Britain except traders, and even they are acquainted only with the sea coast and the areas that are opposite Gaul. And so, although I summoned traders from all parts, I could not find out about the size of the island, the names and populations of the tribes who lived there, their methods of fighting or the customs they had, or which harbours there could accommodate a large number of big ships.[73]

The excuse for intervention was British aid to Gallic resistance, but in any case there were hopes that the island might be rich in gold or silver.[74] Two legions, with cavalry, were considered enough for a reconnaissance expedition.

It was nearly a disaster. The legions had to disembark against fierce opposition (near Deal in Kent), and the main cavalry force never got across the Channel at all. A few days later storms and high tides badly damaged the transport ships, and one of the legions had to be rescued from a dangerously successful ambush. However, Caesar managed to patch up the transports, get his forces safely back to Gaul before the equinox and claim credit for an unprecedented achievement at the very limit of the known world. The Senate, no doubt encouraged by the consuls, Pompey and Crassus, voted a public thanksgiving holiday lasting twenty days.

What the Roman People were giving thanks for was the prospect of yet more conquest to benefit 'the People's thing', the *res publica*. As Cicero once put it, 'the Roman People hate private luxury, but love public magnificence'

– and Cicero was now one of Caesar's friends in Rome, helping to plan the huge programme of public building on which the profits of Caesar's conquests would be spent.[75]

But the dynamic commander still had to deliver the goods. He gave orders for the immediate construction of a large fleet of broad, low-draught transport ships that could easily be beached (he still hadn't found that big safe harbour). He then left for the other end of his province, in modern terms a journey from Boulogne to Dubrovnik, taking in his regular Transpadane assizes on the way, and at the same time composing the fourth of his campaign reports to the People and keeping up a constant stream of effortlessly charming letters to whoever he thought could be usefully influenced. How well it worked can be seen from Cicero's surviving correspondence with his brother Quintus, who was now in Gaul as one of Caesar's deputy commanders:

> What I value most is Caesar's affection for me, which means more to me than all the honours he wants me to expect from him ... I can't have any second thoughts about Caesar. For me he is second only to you and our children, and only just second at that.[76]

Then back to the Ocean, where by July 54 BC an armada of 800 ships was ready to take five legions and 2,000 cavalry across to Kent.

This time the landing was unopposed, and Caesar immediately marched inland. Although the advance wasn't straightforward (storm damage to the ships required a brief return to organise repairs and order replacements), the legions fought their way to the Thames, forced a crossing, penetrated the forests and marshes, and stormed the fortress of the British leader Cassivellaunus. The Britons still had forces in the field (an attack on the Roman base camp had to be beaten off), but the equinox was approaching. It made sense to dictate terms to Cassivellaunus (annual tribute, hostages delivered) and get safely back to Gaul.

The whole of Gaul had been conquered in three campaigning seasons; perhaps the same would be true of Britain? Alternatively, since it turned out that Britain was not, after all, rich in gold and silver, the next great advance might be to the Danube. Meanwhile, Crassus was in Syria preparing for the conquest of Parthia; Pompey, similarly empowered by the People's vote, would be keeping an eye on politics in Rome while his proxy commanders fought in Spain. Cicero had abandoned the *optimates* for the People's cause. It seemed that the old arrogant oligarchy had had its day.

7

Disasters

Caesar is convinced he cannot be safe in Rome if he leaves his army.

> Marcus Caelius Rufus, Roman senator,
> writing to Cicero in 51 BC[77]

In August 54 BC Caesar's daughter Julia, the young wife Pompey doted on, died in childbirth. The reaction of the Roman People was extraordinary. After an emotional funeral ceremony in the Forum, the crowd refused to allow the body to be taken away for private burial. They insisted that she be buried in a grand tomb in the Campus Martius, and when Lucius Domitius, the presiding consul, told them that this would be sacrilegious without a special decree of the Senate, they shouted him down.[78] The Campus Martius was the People's property;[79] Julia was the daughter of the *pontifex maximus*, who was fighting the People's wars at the ends of the earth. Domitius was a wealthy aristocrat and a diehard optimate.[80] Who was he to tell them what to do?

One of Caesar's deputy commanders was contributing to this class-war atmosphere. Lucius Cotta was in charge of one of the legions left in Gaul during the expedition to Britain, and he used his spare time to compose a treatise, *On the Republic*. One brief quotation from it happens to survive, clearly from a passage praising the traditional frugality of the People's commanders:

> Julius Caesar, the first man in history to make the crossing to the islands of Britain, which he did with

a thousand ships [a pardonable exaggeration], took
only three personal servants with him.[81]

How different from the luxurious arrangements of the
arrogant aristocracy!

Just a few months later, Lucius Cotta himself provided
an object lesson in traditional Roman values when he died
fighting to the last alongside his men against the Eburones
in Belgium. It was the worst defeat of the entire Gallic war
– one and a half legions wiped out in a single day. And
it could have been even worse. The legions' winter camps
had been established further apart than usual, making
them vulnerable to individual attacks. Quintus Cicero's
camp was besieged by the Nervii, and only rescued in the
nick of time by Caesar himself.

He would not be going into Italy that winter. The
illusion of Roman invincibility had been dispelled:

As news spread [of the Eburones' victory], almost
all the tribes in Gaul had been discussing the
possibility of going to war; they were sending
messengers and envoys all over the country, finding
out what the other tribes were intending to do and
who would make the first moves in such a war,
and holding meetings at night in deserted places.
Throughout the whole winter there was scarcely a
time when I was not anxious, and receiving some
report or other about plans for a rising among
the Gauls.[82]

In Rome too, politicians were taking note of a changed situation.

Soon the Roman People had even worse news to digest: the abject failure of Crassus' great invasion of Parthia. His defeat at Carrhae, a mere 60 miles east of the Euphrates, was catastrophic. Twenty thousand men were killed, and five out of seven legions lost.[83] Perhaps the Parthians would follow up their victory? It seemed possible that Rome's eastern empire, organised into provinces by Pompey only a few years earlier, might now be lost again.

These calamities were good news for the optimate oligarchs. One of their adversaries was dead, beheaded in the sands of Syria, and Julia's death had broken the link between the other two. Could Pompey be induced to rethink his position?

Caesar was certainly conscious of the danger. Pompey had been recruiting in 'Gaul this side the Alps' for his own Spanish command:

I asked him to mobilise the recruits he had sworn in, and give them orders to march to join me. I wanted to impress public opinion in Gaul not only for the present but for the future as well. It was important to show that our resources in Italy were so great that we could quickly make good any setback we suffered in the war, and even increase the size of our forces. Pompey showed himself to be a patriot and a friend by doing what I asked. [He provided two legions, and a third was raised by Caesar's own recruiting officers.] The size of the reinforcements, and the speed with which they had been assembled, showed what Roman organisation and resources could achieve.[84]

All well and good – but, as it turned out, the Gauls were not so easily discouraged.

In Rome the ideological struggle was now in an acute phase, focused on the ambitions of two rising political stars. Publius Clodius, the *popularis* tribune who had got Cicero exiled five years before, was standing for the praetorship on a very specific programme: to achieve the old aim of 'equal liberty' by abolishing restrictions on the voting rights of freed slaves, arguing that they should be able to vote on the same terms as other citizens. His bitter rival, Titus Milo, who as tribune himself in 57 BC had orchestrated the optimate campaign to get Cicero recalled, was standing for the consulship. Both men's supporters were rowdy and violent, and normal political life was becoming impossible.

Clodius boasted of Caesar's support; Milo staged a threatening demonstration at Caesar's house, the official residence of the *pontifex maximus*.[85] Meanwhile, the *pontifex maximus* himself was using all his legions in remorseless punitive campaigns in Belgium, including another foray across the Rhine into Germany. But there was also unrest among the peoples between the Seine and Loire, which Caesar ruthlessly suppressed by the public execution of Acco, leader of the Senones, and the deployment of six legions at winter camps in their territory. Then back into Italy, for the first time in two years, to hold the assizes and get the latest information from Rome.

The news was bad. On 18 January 52 BC, Milo and Clodius, with their respective escorts, had met on the Appian Way. During a minor fracas in which Clodius was wounded, Milo took the opportunity to finish him off. When the body was brought to Rome and displayed in the Forum, the Roman People, in grief and fury, built Clodius' funeral pyre inside the Senate-house itself, and burned it to the ground in a symbolic act of vengeance.

With rioting in the streets and no magistrates in office except the tribunes (violence had made elections impossible), the Senate authorised Pompey, as holder of a proconsular command, to take the necessary steps to protect the Republic. In particular, all men of military age were to be called up throughout Italy. Caesar immediately recruited two more legions. But he would not be sending them to keep order in Rome.

The exemplary punishment of Acco did not intimidate the Gauls. On the contrary, it spurred them to action. A great new alliance of resistance was formed, led by Vercingetorix, a young noble of the Arverni in the Massif Central. Suddenly, all the Gallic peoples between the Loire and Garonne were united against Rome. Caesar's army was wintering in the north, cut off from its commander (the Cevennes were snowbound and impassable), and the rebels were threatening Provence itself. It looked obvious, both to Vercingetorix and his allies and to Caesar's ill-wishers in Rome, that the conquest of Gaul was about to unravel.

A biography on this scale has to be selective. I cannot begin to do justice to the masterly and audacious campaign waged by Caesar against Vercingetorix in 52 BC – and in any case, no modern account can rival Caesar's own magnificently detailed narrative in the seventh of his *De bello Gallico* commentaries. One of the great classics of the literature of warfare, it vividly attests the ruthless resolve of Caesar as commander and the sheer toughness and tenacity of the men he commanded.

Throughout that year the outcome hung in the balance. There were at least three separate occasions when any rational prognosis would have been for a Gallic victory and the destruction of Caesar and his army. We can be sure that everyone in Rome was desperate to know whether the People's commander would survive, and that quite a few were hoping he wouldn't.

It is important to understand what was at stake. Clodius had been killed in cold blood to prevent his election and the popular legislation that would have followed. The *optimates*, including the incorruptible Marcus Cato,[86] made no secret of their approval of the murder as beneficial to the Republic. As with the Gracchi, Saturninus and Sulpicius, they took it for granted that they would decide which Roman citizen deserved to die, and for what reason. What would they do when Caesar's command expired and he came back to Rome to stand for a second consulship?

The Roman People knew very well what the danger was, and did their best to prevent it. They voted into law a special dispensation allowing Caesar to stand for election *in absentia*, and thus move directly from his provincial command to the consulship. Uniquely, this proposal was sponsored by all ten of the People's tribunes to demonstrate unanimity. Pompey approved, but he probably didn't think it mattered much. After all, there was a good chance that Caesar wouldn't be coming back at all.

Pompey's own position was shifting fast. His new wife, the daughter of an ostentatious aristocrat called Quintus Scipio, was directly descended from the killer of Tiberius Gracchus.[87] Cicero too was moving back to his old optimate allies. He defended Milo on the murder charge, implausibly alleging self-defence; and in the published version of his speech he wrote what he would never have dared to say at the trial itself, before a hostile crowd in the Roman Forum – that Clodius had been no better than a tyrant:

> If Milo *were* the killer of such a man, in admitting it would he have to fear punishment from those he had liberated? … If he *had* done the deed he would admit it – yes, he would admit with pride and pleasure that for the sake of the liberty of all of us he had done what called not just for admission but in truth even for public declaration.[88]

He really meant it. Milo could take pride in killing the People's man, just as Pompey's great-great-grandfather-in-law had done in 133 BC. All it took was a simple slur: 'the man was a tyrant'.

Cicero was an honest man who believed in the rule of law; but he was also thoroughly familiar with Plato's *Republic*, and in particular the passage in book 8 that claims to show how popular freedom leads to tyranny.[89] For him, as for Marcus Cato and Cato's nephew Marcus Brutus, both of whom publicly endorsed the murder of Clodius as a praiseworthy act,[90] Greek philosophy provided a convenient political maxim: all *populares* were tyrants in the making.

Since the fact of murder was inescapable, Milo was found guilty and went into comfortable exile at Marseille, no doubt expecting a triumphant recall, like Cicero's five years earlier, as soon as the oligarchs could arrange it. That didn't happen – and one of the reasons it didn't was the extraordinary bond that long years of warfare had created between Caesar and his legions.

They would do anything for him; and against all the odds, thanks to the heroic endurance and will to prevail that he inspired in them, they succeeded in defeating the huge army amassed from all over Gaul to rescue Vercingetorix from the siege of Alesia. The news reached Rome in the late autumn, by which time Pompey was sharing his third consulship with his new father-in-law. Caesar would be returning after all. The oligarchs were not going to have it all their own way.

In Gaul, the last two years of Caesar's command were an anti-climax. There was plenty of hard fighting still to do, and certainly no chance of new conquests in Britain or the Danube lands, but essentially Gaul was conquered (again), and the People's great new province could be organised and exploited. In Rome, the same two years were a time of ever-increasing tension as the *optimates* manoeuvred to frustrate the People's will and prevent Caesar coming straight back to a second consulship. Pompey, now wholly on the *optimates'* side, regarded it as self-evident that Caesar's consulship would mean the ruin of the Republic, an outcome to be feared above all things.[91] And if it took a civil war to prevent it, well then, 'we shall fight with good hope, either of winning or of dying in freedom'.[92]

It was an assumption that we might nowadays describe as paranoid. For the oligarchs, however, it was axiomatic: Caesar was a *popularis* and therefore a tyrant who would take away their freedom.[93] He must be stopped, by any means.

In December 50 BC the outgoing consuls, with no public authorisation, went to Pompey and instructed him to raise whatever forces were necessary and 'defend the Republic' against Caesar. In January 49 BC, with Pompey's soldiers conspicuous in the Forum, the Senate resolved that, if Caesar did not lay down his command and dismiss his army, he would be regarded as a public enemy. Two of the People's tribunes declared a veto. The Senate then passed an emergency resolution that the magistrates should take whatever steps they saw fit to protect the Republic, and the presiding consul told the tribunes to get out of Rome while they still could. They escaped in a hired carriage disguised as slaves, and headed straight for Ravenna, where Caesar was waiting for news.

Decisive as ever, he marched south at once with the one legion he had. (The others were all in winter camp in Gaul, but messengers were already on their way to summon them.) The story later writers told, that he stopped at the Rubicon boundary and debated whether to cross – 'great evil for the world if I do, and for me if I don't' – is almost certainly a fiction. He already knew what had to be done. The decision had been taken, the dice already thrown.[94]

The *optimates* got their way. The will of the Roman People had been defied, their commander traduced and their tribunes driven out. It is not surprising that the towns of Italy welcomed Caesar. On 21 February, following the capitulation of Lucius Domitius at Corfinium, Caesar spelt out the situation with simple clarity:

> I left my province not for any criminal purpose, but to defend myself against the slanders of my enemies, to restore to their proper place the tribunes of the *plebs* who had been expelled from the city for that reason, and to bring about the freedom of the Roman People, and myself, from oppression by an oligarchic faction.[95]

8

Civil War and Moral Philosophy

I am not disturbed by the fact that those whom I have
released are said to have left the country to make
war against me once more. Nothing pleases me
better than that I should be true to my nature and
they to theirs.

Gaius Julius Caesar,
writing to Cicero in March 49 BC[96]

The last time a Roman proconsul had brought his army into Italy (Lucius Sulla, chapter 3) what followed was the systematic killing of political opponents and the seizure of their property. Sulla's 'proscription' had been a nightmare of terror, and now everyone was afraid it would happen again.

Caesar acted quickly to dispel the fear. He made a point of releasing Domitius and the other high-ranking opponents he had captured at Corfinium, and sent to his friends in Rome a message clearly meant for wide circulation:

> I have decided to show all possible clemency and do my best to reconcile Pompey. Let us try whether by this means we can win back the goodwill of all and enjoy a lasting victory, seeing that others have not managed by cruelty to escape hatred or to make their victories endure – except only Lucius Sulla, whom I do not propose to imitate.[97]

No doubt he knew – as we do, from Cicero's correspondence – that Pompey was in the habit of citing Sulla's example, proscription and all.[98]

The optimate leaders took the same view as Pompey, for their own reasons. Many senior senators, including the two consuls, were with Pompey at Brindisi waiting to cross to Greece with his army. (Pompey's plan was to retreat now and invade Italy later, as Sulla had done.) Cicero, at his villa, heard all about the senators from people who had been there – 'threatening talk about enemies of the *optimates* … nothing but "proscriptions", nothing but "Sulla"!' – and he knew exactly what their motives were:

> Do you suppose there's any criminal act that Scipio, Faustus or Libo wouldn't commit? Their creditors are said to be getting together. Once they've won, what do you think they'll do to their fellow-citizens?[99]

Scipio was Pompey's father-in-law; Libo's daughter was married to Pompey's son Sextus; Faustus was the son of Sulla himself. They *needed* civil war and a ruthless victory or they would be ruined.

Meanwhile, the consuls summoned the Senate to meet in Thessalonica. Since Rome, they said, was in enemy hands, the legitimate government was where they were.[100] A few weeks later, in June 49 BC, Cicero sailed to join them. He was full of misgivings about it, and for good reason. As he explained later to his friend Atticus:

> they had plans for a proscription not by name but by category, and it was their unanimous policy that the spoils of victory would be the possessions of all of you.[101]

Another letter named Lucius Lentulus, the consul who had told the tribunes to get out of Rome; Lentulus had earmarked for himself various post-proscription properties, including Caesar's suburban and Campanian estates.[102] Of course Caesar would have to be safely dead first.

Cicero's evidence is compelling. In the well-informed opinion of one of their own, the men who claimed to be Rome's only legitimate government were characterised by murderous rapacity.

Caesar did not have the ships to pursue Pompey. While a fleet was being put together, he took his forces to Spain to neutralise Pompey's three deputy commanders there, who had a total of seven legions. Again, the military narrative must be left to Caesar's own account in the first two civil war commentaries. Caesar had not bothered to report to the People on his final two years in Gaul (better to leave them with Vercingetorix's surrender), but now he was writing again, and with a difference. The Spanish war was narrated in two separate books, which must mean that the first part, about the Lerida campaign, was written up and sent to Rome during the summer, no doubt in time to enthral the audiences at the Roman Games in September.

Despite what Pompey and the exiled consuls said, the machinery of Senate and People in Rome was still operative. Late in the year the People voted that, in the absence of the consuls, a *dictator* be appointed to hold the elections for the following year. The senior magistrate present, a praetor called Marcus Lepidus (son of the rebel commander of 77 BC), nominated Caesar, and when Caesar got back from Spain he duly presided over the vote.

The People had always wanted him to be consul again; now at last they were able to elect him.

As at Corfinium, so in Spain Caesar had released the opposing commanders unharmed. They went straight to Pompey's headquarters in Greece, where the authority of the consuls and other magistrates who had fled in January was about to expire with the end of the year. By electing their successors – including Caesar, of course – the Roman People had put an end to any doubt about where legitimate government was to be found.

On the fourth day of his consulship, long before the normal sailing season, Caesar managed to get seven legions across the wintry Adriatic. Eight months later, on 9 August 48 BC, now with eight legions against Pompey's eleven, he fought what he hoped would be the decisive battle, at Pharsalus in Thessaly. Afterwards, surveying the thousands of Roman dead, he blamed not Pompey, but the oligarchs who had provoked the war. 'This is what *they* wanted,' he said.[103]

Pompey had preferred escape to surrender and fled to Egypt, but King Ptolemy had him killed as soon as he left the ship. Following with just two under-strength legions, Caesar found himself pinned down in Alexandria in a war between rivals for the Egyptian throne (one of them the young Cleopatra), a side-show that gave the hard-line oligarchs time to regroup.

In Rome, the People did what they could to strengthen their absent consul's hand, voting him the legal authority to make war and peace without consultation and deal with his outlawed enemies as he saw fit; they also granted him the right to be elected consul for each of the next five years, and in the meantime they authorised his nomination as *dictator* for a year.[104] That title may have sounded ominous (chapter 3), but it's clear that the People trusted Caesar not to use his powers in the way Sulla had done. If anyone was going to inflict a new proscription on them it would be the *optimates*, now mustering their forces in North Africa under the very Scipio whose bloodthirsty victory was so dreaded by Cicero. Faustus Sulla was there too.[105]

Back in Rome in the autumn of 47 BC, Caesar left again in December for his next war. On 6 April 46 BC his battle-hardened army routed Scipio at Thapsus (eastern Tunisia). Marcus Cato, determined to allow Caesar no moral credit, killed himself rather than accept his pardon and live in gratitude to his generosity.

Caesar returned again to Rome on 25 July, this time hoping to be able to get down to the urgent business of restoring peace and order. Cicero, a grateful recipient of Caesar's clemency, offered advice on what was necessary and wrote encouragingly to other ex-Pompeians about Caesar's wisdom and magnanimity.[106] Writing a eulogy of Cato, he was needlessly anxious about what the reaction would be; Caesar praised its eloquence and put the opposite case in a two-volume work of his own, recording Cato's 'proud, arrogant, domineering' nature.[107] He was content to let people make up their own minds.

Such tolerance made no difference to the diehards. Pompey's elder son had escaped from the defeat in Africa determined to fight on. By the autumn he had raised a substantial army in Spain, and so in early November

Caesar went to war again. All Cicero's fears returned. He knew from experience what sort of a man young Pompey was, and understood all too well, as he wrote to a friend in January, 'how cruel would be the victory of angry, greedy, arrogant men'.[108] Caesar saved Rome from that, but only at desperate personal risk, seizing a shield and fighting on foot in the front line at the decisive battle in March 45 BC.

Cicero's correspondence again gives us a glimpse of ugly reality, very different from the idealised view of the *optimates* that he was preparing to make public at this very time. In May and June 45 BC he was writing philosophical dialogues, naming each of them, as Plato had done, after the principal participant in the imagined conversation. The *Hortensius* – now lost, but it was the book that changed St Augustine's life[109] – explained how the study of philosophy is essential for living one's life well, and the *Catulus* and *Lucullus* (later renamed *Academica*) exemplified the non-dogmatic methods of Plato's school, 'that ancient philosophy that began with Socrates'.[110]

It was all an invention. Hortensius, Catulus and Lucullus were recently deceased optimate grandees, aristocrats whose knowledge of philosophy had been, at best, rudimentary. As Cicero himself admitted, they couldn't even have dreamed of such erudition.[111] The purpose of the exercise was to present them as cultured gentlemen engaged in rational discussion according to the precepts of 'the most consistent, the most elegant and the least arrogant' of all the philosophical schools.[112]

Cicero knew exactly what his makeover of the oligarchs had to conceal. Hortensius and Lucullus had been notorious for self-indulgent luxury, so he made their literary personae deplore the idea that such behaviour could lead to a life of happiness.[113] Conspicuous consumption was socially divisive. Caesar now brought in sumptuary legislation to control it, and was keen to get back to Rome on a permanent basis to make sure the law was enforced.[114]

The man who inspired and encouraged Cicero's return to literary activity was a new friend, twenty years his junior. He was a fellow optimate, one of those who praised the murder of Clodius, and a fellow enthusiast for the eloquence and wisdom of ancient Athens. He was also an aristocrat, descended from the first consul of the Republic, who led the uprising against the tyrannical Tarquin. He was a nephew of Marcus Cato, and now married to Cato's daughter. His name was Marcus Brutus.

'I have always loved your talents, your interests and your character,' wrote Cicero to Brutus in 46 BC.[115] But that wasn't quite true. Five years earlier, as proconsul of Cilicia (southern Turkey), Cicero had been shocked to hear that the city of Salamis in Cyprus, desperate to raise money to pay the Roman tax collectors, had been lent a huge sum by agents acting for Brutus, at 48 per cent per annum, four times the permitted rate. Not only that, but Brutus had got the previous governor, his then father-in-law, to provide some cavalry squadrons to enforce payment; the city fathers of Salamis were besieged in their Senate-house, where five of their number starved to death.[116]

Writing to Atticus about this scandalous extortion, Cicero made an interesting comment about Brutus himself:

> Even when he has a favour to ask, he normally writes
> in a bullying, arrogant and ungracious manner.[117]

Once more, the survival of private correspondence enables
us to see past the public facade. Brutus wrote a famous
treatise, *On Virtue*, and dedicated it to Cicero; Cicero in
turn dedicated to Brutus his own great dialogues of moral
philosophy, *On Aims* and the *Tusculan Disputations*.[118]
There they were, on public display as scholars and
gentlemen – yet Cicero knew that Brutus could be as
greedy and arrogant as the worst of the optimate oligarchs.

Like Cicero and Cato, Brutus had gone to join Pompey in
Greece when the war broke out. Like Cicero but unlike Cato,
after Pharsalus he gave up opposition and received Caesar's
pardon. Unlike either Cicero or Cato, he accepted high
office from Caesar, becoming governor of 'Gaul this side
the Alps'. (That was the land of the Transpadanes, whom
Caesar had always championed and who now enjoyed the
full citizenship he had promised them years before.) Next
year, in 44 BC, Brutus would be urban praetor in Rome;
nominated by Caesar, his election by the Roman People
would follow as soon as Caesar was back in Rome.

Among his future colleagues in the praetorship was
another up and coming optimate with an ugly history of
provincial profiteering.[119] This was Gaius Cassius, whose
recent trajectory was similarly opportunistic – fighting for
Pompey, then pardoned and promoted by Caesar. Cassius
too had an interest in philosophy, though the school he
favoured was that of Epicurus, who approved of the
pursuit of pleasure.

Cicero wrote to Cassius at the time of the war in Spain, apologising for a short letter with no jokes:

> It's not easy to laugh, but that's the only diversion we have from our troubles. 'Where then,' you will say, 'is philosophy?' Well, yours is in cuisine, but mine is troublesome: I'm ashamed of being a slave, so I find substitution activities for myself. That way I don't hear Plato shouting at me.[120]

A slave? Yes, he meant it. We saw in chapter 5 that when Caesar was first elected consul, the *optimates* regarded his legitimate authority as *regnum*, the power of a king over his subjects, or *dominatio*, the power of a master over his slaves. That was when they knew he would be out of office at the end of the year; this time, the Roman People had voted him successive consulships, and even successive annual dictatorships on top of that.[121] It was power constitutionally granted by the only authority competent to do so – but the *optimates* never accepted that the Roman People had the right to make its own decisions.

The most revealing item in Cicero's brief letter to Cassius is the reference to Plato. Ever since his student days in Athens Cicero had revered Plato, not just as a stylistic paradigm, the fount of all eloquence, but even more as a political thinker.[122] At the great turning points of his career – in June 56 BC when he threw in his lot with Caesar and in March 49 BC when he decided to follow Pompey to Greece – the correspondence reveals him reading Plato for political guidance.[123] So now, even though he was well aware of Caesar's clemency and generosity, what seems to have weighed most on him was the passage in the *Republic* that he called 'Plato on tyrants'.[124] According to Plato, tyranny began with the People's freedom to do as it chose.[125]

Caesar's clemency was strategic as well as tactical. The post-war Republic needed honest and able men in office, and if ex-enemies accepted nomination, so much the better for the future. As Cassius replied to Cicero:

> I hope people will understand how much we hate cruelty and love honesty and clemency, and that good men are getting what bad men most seek and covet. It's hard to persuade people that the right must be chosen for its own sake. But it is both true and demonstrable that pleasure and peace of mind [the aims of Epicureanism] are obtained through virtue, justice and the right.[126]

He clearly hadn't abandoned his philosophical principles. Neither had Brutus, who declared himself happy with Caesar's programme (much to Cicero's disgust) as late as August 45 BC.[127]

But just how honest were they? And what would it take to change their minds?

9

The Oath-Breakers

Do you need to take care lest your enemies plan your death? But who? All those who *were* your enemies have either lost their lives through their own obstinacy or saved them through your leniency. So either you have no enemies left, or those who were are now close friends ... Let me speak for others what I feel myself. Since you think there is some danger to be guarded against, we all promise you not only vigilance and protection but even our own bodies as a physical shield.

Marcus Tullius Cicero, addressing Caesar
in the Senate, September 46 BC[128]

Caesar took care to be back in Rome in time for the start of the Roman Games on 5 September. It mattered that he should receive the grateful applause of the Roman People, but he didn't always pay much attention to the entertainments.[129] There were always letters and reports to dictate or listen to, a huge programme of reform projects to be organised and delegated.

One of the most far-reaching was already complete. The year known as 45 BC was the first of the 'Julian' solar calendar, 365 days long with a leap day to be added every four years. The old lunar calendar had needed regular intercalation, carried out by the college of *pontifices*. But like everything in the *optimates*' republic, it was corrupt:

> Many of the *pontifices*, out of hostility or favour, made longer or shorter intercalations to please themselves, so that some magistrate would have a shorter or longer term of office, or some public contractor make a profit or loss according to the length of the year.[130]

As *pontifex maximus*, Caesar had put a stop to that for the public good.

He wanted to have space as well as time under control. Already in 54 BC he had been interrogating German contacts about the geography of central Europe, and in particular the great Hercynian forest:

> so wide that it would take a man travelling light nine days to cross it; the Germans are unable to describe its width in any other way, for they have no measurements of distance.[131]

That wasn't good enough for the Roman People. If they were to be masters of the world, they needed to measure the world. Caesar commissioned a geographical survey of the whole of Europe, with distances measured. Two or three years later, probably in 51 BC, he added Asia and Africa to the project.[132] Perhaps progress reports from the learned geographers he had put in charge – Theodotus and Didymus for the north and west, Nicodoxus and Polyclitus for the east and south – were among the items engrossing his attention at the Roman Games. It would be another twenty-six years before their world survey was complete.

Caesar was familiar with every province in the Roman People's haphazardly acquired dominions, and he knew how much work would be needed if they were to be more than just an opportunity for private profit. New legislation now limited the tenure of provincial governorships to just one year for ex-praetors and two for ex-consuls. Any senator found guilty of financial abuses on provincial service would be automatically expelled from the Senate.

More generally, since the rich were not deterred by a sentence of exile that might be reversed, all guilty verdicts would now result in the immediate confiscation of half the accused's property.[133] We happen to know that Caesar set great store by these particular laws: the whole republic hung on them, he said.[134]

It was obvious to all that the root of the problem was big money – greed in getting it, extravagance in squandering it, a society fractured between arrogant rich and resentful poor. One adviser put it to Caesar like this:

> You need to strengthen the benefits of concord and drive out the evils of discord. That will happen if you take away the licence to spend and extort, not by re-invoking old statutes, of which the corruption of morals has long since made a mockery, but by insisting that everyone spends within his means. It has become the norm for young men to use up not only their own money but other people's too, to think it splendid never to say no to their own desires or the requests of others, and to regard thoughtlessness as virtue, magnanimity, decency and good behaviour. Fierce self-will takes the path of wickedness, and once fired up, when ordinary resources fail, it turns on our allies [in the provinces] or on our fellow-citizens. That's what destroys stability.[135]

The combination of self-indulgence and self-congratulation was very well observed. This critic's suggestion was to make money lending illegal. Caesar didn't do that, but he did crack down on the divisive display of wealth by taxing the import of luxury goods and restricting the use of extravagant food, clothing and forms of transport.[136]

What mattered to Caesar was public spending to improve the quality of life for the whole citizen body. The great public building programme begun in 54 BC was now well under way. The Roman Forum had been redesigned;[137] it had a grand new basilica, a new Senate-house and speakers' platform, and a huge new colonnaded space – the 'Julian Forum' – presided over by a sumptuous new temple to Venus, the legendary ancestress of the Romans in general and Caesar's family in particular. The Circus Maximus was extended and provided with elaborate permanent seating;[138] two new permanent theatres were planned;[139] the public space for election meetings in the Campus Martius was surrounded with a magnificent rectangular portico, and plans were in hand for the extension of the Campus itself by re-channelling the Tiber further west.[140]

It was not only bricks and mortar. Books were luxury items, and only the very rich could afford libraries. Caesar planned a public collection, with the whole of Greek and Latin literature available to every citizen. He encouraged teachers of the liberal arts as well as medical practitioners to come to Rome by promising them citizenship. Law, too, would be made accessible to the public through the systematic editing of all the Republic's accumulated statutes.[141]

A bronze tablet found in the eighteenth century reveals the thoroughness of Caesar's own legislative initiatives:

among other things, the text contains regulations for the upkeep and permitted use of roads, porticos and other public spaces; standing orders for local government in at least one Italian municipality; and arrangements for the collection and delivery to Rome of local census data.[142] Administrative propriety was fundamental.

Caesar conducted a mini-census in the city of Rome itself in order to discover exactly who was entitled to receive the subsidised grain ration introduced by Gaius Gracchus. The *optimates* always complained about that urban welfare programme – Cicero referred contemptuously to 'the wretched starving *plebs*, bloodsuckers of the public purse'[143] – but, as we saw in chapter 2, it was their own greed for great estates, forcing small farmers off the land, that had made it necessary in the first place. Now Caesar was reversing the effect. He cut the list of recipients from 320,000 to 150,000, and provided 80,000 citizens with farming land in colonial settlements overseas.[144]

Two of those settlements involved the rebuilding of historic cities. Carthage and Corinth had been destroyed by the Romans a century before and their territories abandoned – now they would live again as Roman cities for Roman citizens. Corinth's strategic position would be enhanced by the construction of a canal through the isthmus. In Italy, too, great infrastructure projects were on Caesar's agenda: a new road across the Apennines to the Adriatic; a new harbour at Ostia; the draining of the Fucine lake to provide 160 sq. km of fertile farming land; the draining of the Pontine marshes, incorporating a new channel for the Tiber that would bring ocean-going vessels up from Tarracina.[145]

On top of all that, the eastern empire had to be made secure by a new war against Parthia. But, as Caesar's biographer succinctly put it, 'these schemes were cancelled by his assassination'.[146]

Serious reform requires time and patience. In the Roman Republic, where tenure of legislative office lasted only a year, the time needed for planning and implementation could only be achieved by political compromise and a willingness to co-operate for the public good – virtues not seen in Rome for three generations. Ever since the murder of Tiberius Gracchus polarised political ideology, *popularis* reformers could count on fierce obstruction during their term of office and the likely reversal of their legislation as soon as the year was over.

The Roman People understood the problem very well; they tried to counter it by voting Caesar successive consulships in advance, and then doing the same thing with the emergency office of *dictator*. So on 1 January 44 BC Caesar became consul for the fifth time, with Marcus Antonius ('Antony') as his colleague, and *dictator* for the fourth time, with Marcus Lepidus as his deputy. He had already been voted ten future consulships, and early in the year he was made *dictator perpetuus*, the emergency office now effectively permanent. The institutions of the republic were being stretched to breaking point.

There were some who thought that Caesar's unique authority as the People's champion would be better defined by a return to monarchy. After all, six of the seven Roman kings had ruled by the vote and consent of the People; only Tarquin, the last of them, had seized power by force and ruled as a despot. But Caesar forcefully rejected the idea. After Tarquin's expulsion the Romans had sworn never to have a king again, and he would not incur the gods' wrath by allowing that oath to be broken.[147]

Perhaps appeal to divine sanction was the only way out of the impasse. In January 44 BC the Roman People voted Caesar the sacrosanctity that protected their tribunes.[148] Any violence offered to him would be an offence against the gods – a sacrilege punishable by death. But that protection hadn't helped Tiberius Gracchus (chapter 2), Lucius Saturninus or Publius Sulpicius (chapter 3). More ruthless than the patricians of the early Republic (chapter 1), the modern oligarchy had repeatedly committed sacrilegious murder and got away with it. Something more was needed.

Caesar dismissed his bodyguard once the triumphal parade for his Spanish victory was over. Now the civil wars were finished, there should be no need for an armed guard. Instead, every senator and every member of the equestrian order took an oath to protect him: 'if anyone should conspire against him, those who failed to defend him were to be accursed.'[149] Caesar knew the risk he was running. In the end, it was a gamble on the *optimates'* patriotism:

It is more important for Rome than for myself that I should survive. I have long been sated with power and glory; but should anything happen to me, Rome will enjoy no peace. A new civil war will break out under far worse conditions than the last.[150]

It was also a gamble on their gratitude. Caesar had spared his enemies' lives and promoted some of them to high office; indeed, the two senior praetors in 44 BC were Marcus Brutus and Gaius Cassius, those connoisseurs of Greek moral philosophy.

The gamble failed on both counts. All that mattered to the oligarchs was the free play of ambition: the chance of gaining lucrative office without restriction. A contemporary scholar and historian described their irresponsibility from personal knowledge:

> Most of them have been infected by such a lust for office that they'd be happy for the sky to fall, just so long as they get their magistracy.[151]

As for gratitude, 'Plato on tyranny' trumped all of Caesar's clemency and generosity. They had decided he was a tyrant, and that was enough.

More than sixty men chose to break their oath and bring about his murder. The man they picked as their leader and spokesman was Marcus Brutus, proud descendant of the Lucius Brutus who led the rising against Tarquin 463 years earlier. They too were going to be heroic liberators.

They would do the deed as senators. On 15 March the Senate met in the hall attached to Pompey's theatre and portico. When Caesar, who was presiding, came in and sat down, he was immediately surrounded by the principal conspirators. Our various sources name nine of them, but there may have been more. The first to strike was Lucius Casca from behind Caesar's left shoulder, and when Caesar half-rose and turned to grab Casca's arm the others drew their daggers and attacked. Afterwards, twenty-three wounds were counted on the corpse.[152]

Unarmed, surrounded and defiant, Caesar was killed 'like a trapped wild animal'.[153] As the terrified senators ran for their lives, the shouting panicked the crowd outside in the portico and theatre, where everyone had been watching a gladiatorial show. The assassins came out, their bloodstained weapons in their hands, and Brutus tried to call for calm: 'Don't be afraid! Nothing bad has happened!' But no one was listening. Everyone fled – except the gladiators, who now presented themselves for duty as the conspirators had pre-arranged.[154] Guarded by them, Brutus and the others made their way to the Forum, shouting that they had freed the republic and killed the tyrant. But there were no cheering crowds.

'When the People did not run to join them, the assassins were disconcerted and afraid.'[155] The conspirators retreated to the Capitol, still protected by their gladiators, and in due course Antony as consul restored order in the streets and negotiated a truce. Only then did the fearful citizens dare to make their voices heard. They had two urgent but incompatible points to make: they wanted peace and they wanted vengeance.[156]

The second demand outweighed the first, and was angrily repeated at Caesar's funeral. When Antony got the herald to recite all the honours for Caesar that the People had voted into law, including that of sacrosanctity, and the words of the oath that all the senators had sworn to protect him, there was a furious reaction from the crowd.[157] How had the assassins so totally misjudged the People's will? Perhaps they were just so arrogant that they knew it and didn't care.

That is certainly the impression one gets from Cicero's letters, where the dead man is referred to as a tyrant, the assassins as heroes and the murder as the most glorious of deeds.[158] One of Caesar's friends, protesting at this language, complained that the *optimates* even objected to his grief:

> I'm well aware of what they've said against me since Caesar's death. They consider it an offence that I find it hard to bear the death of a friend, and that I'm angry that someone I loved has died. They say patriotism should be put before friendship – as if they've already proved that his death was of benefit to the republic … 'You'll suffer for it, then,' they say, 'for daring to disapprove of what we did.' What unheard-of arrogance![159]

That is a precious document. Without it, we might be tempted to take Cicero's view as the norm, rather than a partisan expression of ideological prejudice.

It may also be worth noting the verdict of a historian writing two and a half centuries later. Cassius Dio was a senior senator who had lived through the reigns of Commodus and Caracalla, and therefore knew something about tyrannical rulers. This is how he introduced his account of the Ides of March:

> While Caesar was preparing for his campaign against the Parthians, an accursed madness fell on certain men who were jealous of his pre-eminence and resentful that he outranked them in honour. That lawless madness killed him, adding a new name to the record of infamy; it tore up constitutional votes and turned the Romans' state of harmony into conflicts and civil wars. They said they were overthrowing Caesar and liberating the People, but in fact they treacherously plotted against him and brought conflict to a city that was now well governed.[160]

Blaming it on madness may be too easy, but otherwise it is a judgement that deserves respect.

10

Hail, Caesar

At the age of nineteen, on my own initiative and at my own expense, I raised an army with which I brought about the freedom of the republic from oppression by a dominant faction ... In the year when both consuls had fallen in war [43 BC], the People elected me consul, and *triumuir* for the establishment of the republic. I avenged the crime of those who killed my father by driving them into exile through the courts of law, and then by defeating them twice in battle when they made war on the republic [42 BC].

Imperator Caesar Augustus (63 BC–AD 14), son of Divus Julius.[161]

Caesar's will was made public a few days after the murder. He had named his great-nephew Gaius Octavius as his principal heir, and 'adopted him into his family and his name'.[162] It was a brilliant choice.

Young Octavius, now young Caesar, was not physically robust, but he had mental toughness, tenacity and a powerful belief in his own destiny. Not long after he came to Rome to claim his perilous inheritance, a comet was visible for seven days in the northern sky. As he noted later in his memoirs, the People believed it meant that the soul of Caesar had been received among the immortal gods. But he was sure it was meant for *him*, signifying his own rebirth as Caesar.[163]

He was ruthless enough, with his triumviral colleagues, to visit on the *optimates* the proscriptions and summary executions they themselves had threatened. Remember how Caesar's clemency and generosity had been abused?[164] The *triumuiri* were elected and empowered by the Roman People, and the People were in no mood to be merciful. You might say the oligarchs had it coming.

Fifteen years later, in 29 BC, after years of brutal warfare, hardship and ruin for many thousands of Romans, the not-so-young Caesar (he was 33) returned to a Rome exhausted but at peace. He came back with the spoils of

Cleopatra's Egypt, the last and richest of the Hellenistic kingdoms, now 'in the power of the Roman People'.[165] As soon as his triumphal games were over, he dedicated the temple of Divus Julius, built in the Forum at the spot where the People had built the funeral pyre fifteen years earlier. Julius Caesar was now one of the gods.

Traumatised by constant civil war, the Romans were desperate for a new start. Now at last they had it:

> In my sixth and seventh consulships [28 and 27 BC], after I had extinguished the civil wars, being with universal consent in complete control of affairs, I transferred the republic from my own power to the dominion of the Senate and the Roman People. For this benefit I was called 'Augustus' by decree of the Senate.[166]

The name alluded to the 'august augury' by which the gods confirmed the original Roman People's grant of authority to Romulus.[167] What Caesar Augustus had done was give 'the People's thing' back to its true owners, and they in turn empowered him.

He was not an 'emperor'. There was no palace, no throne and no regalia. The Latin *imperator* means 'military commander', and the military command (*imperium*) that the Senate and People voted him was limited in both space and time – though, of course, they hoped it would be renewed, as indeed it was. A few years later they gave him the powers of the People's tribunes, not restricted, as theirs were, to the city of Rome but empire wide. That was explicitly for the protection of ordinary people,[168] and what it meant can be seen from the words of a poet in around 13 BC:

While Caesar is the guardian of our affairs, no civil madness or violence will drive out peace, nor anger that forges swords and brings wretched cities to enmity.[169]

Rome valued the pre-eminence of Caesar Augustus because it kept the greedy and arrogant under control.

Augustus lived long, and presided over an era his contemporaries called a golden age. He thought of his role as 'guard duty' (*statio*), and he hoped to hand it on to a son of his own.[170] In the end he had to adopt his stepson, a man who thought like an old-fashioned optimate, and the results were predictably unhappy. But the principle had been established: his unique pre-eminence could be, and was, formally handed on to a successor.

It was a return to monarchy, but of a very particular kind. Augustus' successors were not kings or *dictators* – they were *Caesars*, and what that meant can best be seen from the events of AD 41. When Augustus' great-grandson, the appalling Caligula, was killed by his own guards officers, the senators thought the 'tyranny of the Caesars' was over and they were in charge again. But, as a well-informed historian tells us:

the People resented the Senate; they saw the emperors as a curb on its arrogant behaviour and a protection for themselves. They were delighted at the seizure of Claudius [by the Praetorian Guard], believing that if he became emperor he would save them from the sort of civil strife there had been in the days of Pompey.[171]

Since Claudius had no right to the name 'Caesar' by either birth or adoption, his assumption of it was an epoch-making moment. The name had become a title.

• • •

What, no '*ueni, uidi, uici*', no 'Caesar's wife must be above suspicion', no '*et tu, Brute*'? I'm afraid not: I wanted to stick to what is important. Readers can find those and other anecdotes in the works listed below as Further Reading – where they will also find much more sympathetic treatments of the Roman aristocracy and the men who called themselves the liberators.

I think modern historians are much too ready to take the murderous *optimates* at their own self-flattering estimation. Readers can make up their own minds about that, and to help them I've provided references to primary sources for all controversial views. There is, in fact, an astonishing amount of material available for the world of Julius Caesar 2,000 years ago, but it's not straightforward to bring it together and make sense of it all.

Why does it matter? Well, however deplorable imperialism may be, the Roman Empire was a coherent military and fiscal system that for four centuries provided western Europe, north Africa and the Middle East with security, prosperity and relative peace. It imposed on

Europe a literate urban society, the memory and example of which made possible what we call 'western civilisation'. And it could not have happened without Julius Caesar.

Geographically, the empire was largely created by the People's champions: Pompey in western Asia (66–62 BC), Caesar himself in Gaul (58–50 BC), Augustus in the Balkans (15–9 BC). But how would it be exploited, and for whose benefit? It took all of Caesar's vision, toughness and relentless energy to claim back 'the People's thing' from the oligarchs who would have made it a mere kleptocracy. And they killed him for it.

A Giant? Yes, I think we can say he was.

Notes

Except where otherwise stated, all translations are the author's.

1. Eratosthenes, quoted in Strabo, *Geography* 1.4.9 (C66).
2. Dionysius of Halicarnassus, *Roman Antiquities* 2.7.4.
3. Ibid. 2.15.3–4, 2.28.3.
4. Livy, *Ab urbe condita* 2.1.1.
5. Appian, *Civil Wars* 1.1.1.
6. Livy, *Ab urbe condita* 4.5.1.
7. Manius Curius, quoted in Columella, *Res rustica* 1.pref.14, 1.3.10, and Frontinus, *Stratagems* 4.3.12.
8. Cornelius Nepos, *Life of Cato* 3.4; Pliny, *Natural History* 8.11.
9. Livy, *Ab urbe condita* 34.54.5–7.
10. Polybius, *Histories* 1.1.5.
11. Ibid. 6.18.2–3 (concord), 6.54.3–6 (sacrifice for public good), 6.56.2 (bribery disgraceful), 6.56.14–15 (behaviour in office).
12. *First Book of Maccabees* 1.8.1, 1.8.12–16 (trans. *New English Bible*).
13. Sallust, *Catiline* 10.4.
14. Funeral oration for Lucius Metellus, consul in 251 and 247 BC, quoted in Pliny, *Natural History* 7.140.

15. Sallust, *Jugurthine War* 63.6–7.
16. Ibid. 5.1–2.
17. Appian, *Civil Wars* 1.11.44; Siculus Flaccus, *De condicionibus agrorum* 102.29–33 (ed. Brian Campbell, 2000).
18. Cicero, *In Catilinam* 1.4.
19. Cicero, *Pro Sestio* 96.
20. Cicero, *De republica* 3.23.
21. Quoted in Charisius, *Ars grammatica* 2.240.
22. Gaius Memmius, as impersonated by Sallust, *Jugurthine War* 31.12–13.
23. Plutarch, *Life of Marius* 23.6.
24. Ibid. 27.5.
25. Sulla, quoted in Plutarch, *Life of Caesar* 1.2.
26. Tacitus, *Dialogus* 28.5; Cicero, *Brutus* 252.
27. Seneca, *Epistulae morales* 94.
28. Cicero, *Brutus* 261; Quintilian, *Institutio oratoria* 10.1.114.
29. Anon., *Rhetorica ad Herennium* 4.31; Plutarch, *Life of Marius* 35.1.
30. Appian, *Civil Wars* 1.57.253.
31. Dionysius of Halicarnassus, *Roman Antiquities* 5.70; Appian, *Civil Wars* 1.3.9–10, 1.98–9.459–62.
32. Cicero, *Pro Roscio Amerino* 136.
33. Suetonius, *Life of Caesar* 2–3; Pliny, *Natural History* 16.11–12.
34. Sallust, *Histories* 1.77.21–2; Florus 2.11.6.
35. Ibid. 3.48.9 ('more cruel than Sulla').
36. Ibid. 4.69.20 (letter of Mithridates to Arsaces of Parthia).

37. Cicero, *In Verrem* 1, gives a vivid contemporary account.
38. Plutarch, *Life of Caesar* 4.2–3 (trans. Rex Warner, 1958).
39. Cicero, *In Catilinam* 4.4.
40. Cicero, *In Verrem* 1.11; Tacitus, *Annals* 11.22.6.
41. Plutarch, *Life of Caesar* 5.1–2.
42. Pliny, *Letters* 1.14.4–6.
43. Plutarch, *Life of Caesar* 6 (trans. Christopher Pelling, 2011).
44. Suetonius, *Life of Caesar* 16.2.
45. Quoted in Pliny, *Natural History* 7.97, and Plutarch, *Life of Pompey* 45.3.
46. Cicero, *Ad Atticum* 2.3.3–4 (trans. L.P. Wilkinson, 1949).
47. Ibid. 2.1.6–7.
48. Livy, *Ab urbe condita* 2.32.8–12; Dionysius of Halicarnassus, *Roman Antiquities* 6.83.2 ('in all the old historians').
49. Sallust, *Catiline* 34.1; Lucius Crassus (consul 95 BC), quoted in Cicero, *De oratore* 1.225.
50. Marcus Antonius (consul 91 BC), as impersonated in Cicero, *De oratore* 1.226.
51. Explicit in Cicero, *Ad Atticum* 4.3.3.
52. Cicero, *De officiis* 3.32.
53. Cassius Dio, *Roman History* 38.1.3 (trans. E. Cary, 1914).
54. Livy, *Ab urbe condita* 39.40.9–11.
55. Cassius Dio, *Roman History* 38.3.1 (trans. E. Cary, 1914).

56. Ibid. 38.4.2–4.
57. Cicero, *Ad Atticum* 1.19.4 (landowners); 2.12.1, 2.13.2 (*regnum*); 2.14.1, 2.17.1 (tyranny); 2.18.1–2 (slavery and oppression).
58. Ibid. 2.20.3.
59. Sallust, *Histories* 4.69.22.
60. Justinian, *Digest of Roman Law* 48.11 (AD 534).
61. Plutarch, *Life of Caesar* 14.5.
62. Strabo, *Geography* 7.3.5, 7.3.11.
63. Caesar, *De bello Gallico* 1.44.12 (reported by Ariovistus himself).
64. Cicero, *Ad Quintum fratrem* 2.16.4 (trans. D.R. Shackleton Bailey, 1978).
65. Anon., *Demonstratio artis geometricae* 395–6 (ed. K. Lachmann, 1848–52).
66. Pliny, *Natural History* 7.91.
67. Asconius, *Commentary on Cicero* 46–7 (ed. A.C. Clark, 1907); Cassius Dio, *Roman History* 38.30.3.
68. Plutarch, *Life of Caesar* 17.3.
69. Cicero, *De finibus* 5.52.
70. Attested in Sallust, *Catiline* 54.2–3, and Suetonius, *Life of Caesar* 28.1.
71. Cicero, *Philippics* 1.36 ('The entire Roman People'); Pliny, *Natural History* 36.120.
72. Caesar, *De bello Gallico* 4.16.1.
73. Ibid. 4.20.3–4.
74. Cicero, *Ad familiares* 7.7.1, *Ad Atticum* 4.16.7.
75. Cicero, *Pro Murena* 76; *Ad Atticum* 4.16.7–8 (July 54 BC).
76. Cicero, *Ad Quintum fratrem* 2.14.1, 3.1.18 (June and September 54 BC).

77. Cicero, *Ad familiares* 8.14.2.

78. Cassius Dio, *History of Rome* 39.64; Plutarch, *Life of Pompey* 53.2–4.

79. Aulus Gellius, *Noctes Atticae* 7.7.4; *Digest of Roman Law* 18.1.6.1.

80. Cicero, *Pro Milone* 22; [Sallust], *Ad Caesarem senem* 2.4.2.

81. Quoted in Athenaeus, *Deipnosophistae* 6.273b.

82. Caesar, *De bello Gallico* 5.53.4–5.

83. Plutarch, *Life of Crassus* 20.1 (legions), 31.7 (casualties).

84. Caesar, *De bello Gallico* 6.1.2–4.

85. Cicero, *Pro Milone* 66, 88.

86. Asconius, *Commentary on Cicero* 54 (ed. A.C. Clark, 1907).

87. Caesar, *De bello Gallico* 1.4.3 (ostentation); Cicero, *Ad Atticum* 6.1.17 (descent).

88. Cicero, *Pro Milone* 79–80.

89. Cicero, *De republica* 1.66-8 (54–53 BC), paraphrasing Plato, *Republic* 8.562c–566d.

90. Asconius, *Commentary on Cicero* 41, 53–4 (ed. A.C. Clark, 1907).

91. Quoted in Cicero, *Ad Atticum* 7.8.4, 7.9.3 (December 50 BC).

92. Ibid. 7.9.4.

93. Ibid. 7.5.4 (December 50 BC), 7.11.1 (January 49 BC), etc.

94. Suetonius, *Life of Caesar* 32 (*'iacta alea est'*).

95. Caesar, *De bello ciuili* 1.22.5.

96. Quoted in Cicero, *Ad Atticum* 9.16.2 (trans. D.R. Shackleton Bailey, 1968).

97. Ibid. 9.7c.1 (trans. Shackleton Bailey, slightly adapted).

98. Ibid. 9.7.3, 9.10.2 ('Sulla could do it, so can't I?'), 9.10.6 (proscription), 10.7.1.

99. Ibid. 9.11.3–4 (20 March 49 BC).

100. Cassius Dio, *Roman History* 41.18.5, 41.43.2–3.

101. Cicero, *Ad Atticum* 11.6.2; similarly *Ad familiares* 4.9.3, 6.6.6, 7.3.2, and *Pro Marcello* 16.

102. Cicero, *Ad Atticum* 11.6.6.

103. Asinius Pollio, quoted in Suetonius, *Life of Caesar* 30.4.

104. Cassius Dio, *Roman History* 42.20–1.

105. Cicero, *Ad Atticum* 9.11.4; Cassius Dio, *Roman History* 42.13.3–44.

106. Cicero, *Pro Marcello* 12–18 (clemency), 23–4 (advice); *Ad familiares* 4.4.4, 6.6.10 etc. (autumn 46 BC).

107. Cicero, *Ad Atticum* 12.4.2, 13.46.1; Aulus Gellius, *Noctes Atticae* 4.16.8.

108. Cicero, *Ad familiares* 4.14.2 (January 45 BC).

109. Augustine, *Confessions* 3.4.7–8.

110. Cicero, *Ad Atticum* 3.32.3, *De diuinatione* 2.1, *Academica* 1.2.

111. Cicero, *Ad Atticum* 13.16.1, 13.19.5.

112. Cicero, *De diuinatione* 2.1.

113. Varro, *De re rustica* 3.17.5–9; Plutarch, *Life of Lucullus* 39–41; Cicero, *Hortensius,* quoted in Augustine, *De uita beata* 4.26.

114. Cicero, *Ad Atticum* 13.7 (June 45 BC).

115. Cicero, *Orator* 33.

116. Cicero, *Ad Atticum* 5.21.10–13, 6.1.2–8, 6.2.7–9 (February–April 50 BC).

117. Ibid. 6.1.7.
118. Cicero, *De finibus* 1.8, *Tusculan Disputations* 5.1.
119. Anon., *De uiris illustribus* 83.2 (as quaestor in Syria, 51 BC).
120. Cicero, *Ad familiares* 15.18.1 (December 46 BC).
121. Cassius Dio, *Roman History* 42.20.3 (after Pharsalus), 43.14.4 (after Thapsus).
122. E.g. Cicero, *Ad Atticum* 2.1.8 ('our god, Plato'); *Orator* 10–15 (eloquence); *Ad Quintum fratrem* 1.1.29, *De officiis* 1.85 (politics).
123. Cicero, *Ad familiares* 1.9.12, 1.9.18, *Ad Atticum* 9.13.4.
124. Cicero, *Ad Atticum* 10.8.6 (May 49 BC).
125. Plato, *Republic* 8.562b–c, 563d–e, 569c.
126. Cicero, *Ad familiares* 15.9.2 (January 45 BC).
127. Cicero, *Ad Atticum* 13.40.1.
128. Cicero, *Pro Marcello* 21, 35.
129. Cicero, *Ad Atticum* 13.45.1 (back in time); Suetonius, *Life of Augustus* 45.1 (inattention).
130. Censorinus, *De die natali* 20.7.
131. Caesar, *De bello Gallico* 6.25.1.
132. Dates inferred from 'Aethicus', *Cosmographia* 1–2 (ed. Alexander Riese, 1877).
133. Cassius Dio, *Roman History* 43.25.3; Suetonius, *Life of Caesar* 42.3, 43.1.
134. Quoted in Cicero, *Philippics* 1.24.
135. 'Sallust', *Epistulae ad Caesarem* 1.5.4–6.
136. Suetonius, *Life of Caesar* 43.1–2.
137. Cassius Dio, *Roman History* 43.49.1; Pliny, *Natural History* 15.78.

138. Pliny, *Natural History* 36.102; Dionysius of Halicarnassus, *Roman Antiquities* 3.68.2–4.

139. Cassius Dio, *Roman History* 43.49.2, 53.30.5 (the later Theatre of Marcellus); Suetonius, *Life of Caesar* 44.1.

140. Cicero, *Ad Atticum* 4.16.8, 13.33.4.

141. Suetonius, *Life of Caesar* 42.1 (teachers and doctors), 44.2 (library and law edition).

142. *Roman Statutes* 24.20–158 (ed. M.H. Crawford, 1996).

143. Cicero, *Ad Atticum* 1.16.11.

144. Suetonius, *Life of Caesar* 41.3, 42.1.

145. Cassius Dio, *Roman History* 43.50.3–5 (Carthage and Corinth); Plutarch, *Life of Caesar* 58.4–5 (Ostia, Tiber); Suetonius, *Life of Caesar* 44.3.

146. Suetonius, *Life of Caesar* 44.4 (trans. Robert Graves, 1957).

147. Appian, *Civil Wars* 2.107.444.

148. Ibid. 2.106.442; Cassius Dio, *Roman History* 44.5.3.

149. Appian, *Civil Wars* 2.145.604 (trans. John Carter, 1996).

150. Quoted in Suetonius, *Life of Caesar* 86.2 (trans. Robert Graves, 1957).

151. Varro, *De uita populi Romani* (44 or 43 BC), quoted in Nonius Marcellus, *De compendiosa doctrina* 802 (ed. W.M. Lindsay, 1903).

152. Suetonius, *Life of Caesar* 82.2; Appian, *Civil Wars* 4.8.34.

153. Plutarch, *Life of Caesar* 66.6.

154. Nicolaus of Damascus, *Life of Caesar* 91–2 (ed. Felix Jacoby, 1925); Appian, *Civil Wars* 2.118.494–5.

155. Appian, *Civil Wars* 2.119.501.
156. Ibid. 2.130–1.542–51.
157. Ibid. 2.144–5.602–4.
158. Cicero, *Ad Atticum* 14.4.2, 14.5.2, 14.6.1–2 (10–12 April 44 BC), and constantly thereafter.
159. Gaius Matius, in Cicero, *Ad familiares* 11.28.2–3 (autumn 44 BC).
160. Cassius Dio, *Roman History* 44.1.1–2.
161. Augustus, *Res gestae* 1–2.
162. Suetonius, *Life of Caesar* 83.2.
163. Pliny, *Natural History* 2.94.
164. Appian, *Civil Wars* 4.8.31–4 (Triumvirs' edict).
165. The proper formula: e.g. Macrobius, *Saturnalia* 1.12.35.
166. Augustus, *Res gestae* 34.1–2.
167. Suetonius, *Life of Augustus* 2; Dionysius of Halicarnassus, *Roman Antiquities* 2.4–6.
168. Tacitus, *Annals* 1.2.1.
169. Horace, *Odes* 4.15.17–20.
170. Augustus, quoted in Aulus Gellius, *Noctes Atticae* 15.7.3.
171. Josephus, *Jewish Antiquities* 19.228.

Timeline

Further Reading

Alston, Richard, *Rome's Revolution: Death of the Republic and Birth of the Empire* (Oxford University Press, 2015)

Billows, Richard A., *Julius Caesar: The Colossus of Rome* (Routledge, 2009)

Crook, J.A., Lintott, Andrew and Rawson, Elizabeth (eds), *The Cambridge Ancient History*, second edition: Vol. 9, *The Last Age of the Roman Republic 146–43 BC* (Cambridge University Press, 1994)

Gelzer, Matthias, *Caesar: Politician and Statesman* (Blackwell, 1968)

Goldsworthy, Adrian, *Caesar: The Life of a Colossus* (Weidenfeld & Nicolson, 2006)

Griffin, Miriam (ed.), *A Companion to Julius Caesar* (Wiley-Blackwell, 2009)

Harris, Robert, *Dictator* (Hutchinson, 2015)

Holland, Tom, *Rubicon: The Triumph and Tragedy of the Roman Republic* (Little, Brown Book Group, 2003)

Meier, Christian, *Caesar* (HarperCollins, 1995)

Pelling, Christopher, *Plutarch Caesar, Translated with an Introduction and Commentary* (Oxford University Press, 2011)

Seager, Robin, *Pompey the Great: A Political Biography* (Blackwell, 2002)

Stevenson, Tom, *Julius Caesar and the Transformation of the Roman Republic* (Routledge, 2015)

Strauss, Barry, *The Death of Caesar: The Story of History's Most Famous Assassination* (Simon & Schuster, 2015)

Tatum, W. Jeffrey, *Always I am Caesar* (Blackwell, 2006)

Welch, Kathryn, and Powell, Anton (eds), *Julius Caesar as Artful Reporter: The War Commentaries as Political Instruments* (Duckworth, 1998)

Wiseman, T.P., *Remembering the Roman People* (Oxford University Press, 2009)

Wiseman, T.P., 'The Many and the Few', *History Today* 64.8 (2014) 10–15

Wyke, Maria, *Caesar: A Life in Western Culture* (University of Chicago Press, 2008)

Digital Resources

http://classicsresources.info/
https://wiki.digitalclassicist.org/Main_Page
http://dcc.dickinson.edu/caesar/caesar-introduction
http://orbis.stanford.edu/
http://penelope.uchicago.edu/Thayer/E/Roman/home.
    html
www.perseus.tufts.edu/hopper/collections

pocket GIANTS

A series about people who changed the world –
and why they matter.

Series Editor – Tony Morris

www.thehistorypress.co.uk

Lightning Source UK Ltd.
Milton Keynes UK
UKOW06f1132021116

286691UK00010B/107/P